The Nuclear Dilemma in American Strategic Thought

D0068661

About the Book and Author

Since the end of World War II, the United States has faced moral and strategic issues in its management of force that are unique in the history of international politics. At the heart of these issues is the heavy reliance of the United States and its allies on the deterrent effect of nuclear weapons and the fact that their use would very likely lead to self-defeating destruction and ecological catastrophe. This dilemma affects every major military decision and strategic debate, and the history of U.S. strategic thought can be viewed as an attempt to cope by rejecting, abolishing, or mitigating the nuclear specter.

In this incisive review, Dr. Osgood explores the evolution of postwar strategic thought in the United States, examining the moral and practical implications of the nuclear dilemma in a masterly synthesis of all aspects of the nuclear deterrence debate. His discussion of the issues is both a personal essay by a participant in the debate and a major contribution to the development of strategic thought in the future.

Robert E. Osgood was, at the time of his death in 1986, Christian A. Herter Professor of American Foreign Policy and co-director of the security studies program at the Johns Hopkins University School of Advanced International Studies (SAIS).

The Nuclear Dilemma in American Strategic Thought

Robert E. Osgood

Westview Press • Boulder and London

This book is an expanded version of a contribution to the research project "Political Rationales and Moral Justification for Nuclear Deterrence," which the Stiftung Wissenschaft und Politik (SWP) is conducting with support from the Ford Foundation. The project findings will be published eventually in two volumes.

Copyright © 1988 by Westview Press, Inc.

Published in 1988 in the United States of America by Westview Press, Inc.; Frederick A. Praeger, Publisher: 5500 Central Avenue, Boulder, Colorado 80301

Library of Congress Cataloging-in-Publication Data
Osgood, Robert Endicott.
    The nuclear dilemma in American strategic thought.
    Includes index.
    1. United States—Military policy. 2. Nuclear warfare. 3. Deterrence (Strategy). I. Title.
UA23.082 1988   355'.0335'73   87-21661
ISBN 0-8133-0537-3

Printed and bound in the United States of America

⊗   The paper used in this publication meets the requirements of the American National Standard for Permanence of Paper for Printed Library Materials Z39.48-1984.

10   9   8   7   6   5   4   3   2

For Elaine

Contents

Foreword

American attitudes toward world politics and particularly the use of military power were always close to the center of Robert E. Osgood's interests. His first major work, *Ideals and Self-Interest in America's Foreign Relations,* was a searching interpretative essay on the evolution of the American outlook toward the world during the half-century prior to World War II. It was a period of great change in the nation's international position. In analyzing the debates that attended this change, Professor Osgood traced the growth of political realism in the United States. He pointed out that an extraordinary transformation had occurred and that it had largely been the result of the fear of national insecurity. At the same time, he argued that although this fear had been the indispensable condition for the growth of political realism, it was not realism itself, and that, accordingly, the persistence of insecurity was no guarantee of the triumph of realism in foreign policy. Rather than promoting realism, insecurity might give rise to illusions quite as dangerous as those that in an earlier period resulted from the assurance of an exaggerated sense of security. Although a widespread political realism formed the indispensable balance wheel of a foreign policy that effectively responded to the nation's interests, there was no ready formula for achieving it, just as there was no final solution to the problem of determining the changing requirements of interest.

Ideals and Self-Interest in America's Foreign Relations was written at the beginning of the post–World War II period. Although it was clear that the United States would not revert to its isolationist past, the habits and outlook formed during this past were still very much with us, and Osgood's effort was largely directed at countering their remaining influence. His appeal was to the nation's "own enlightened self-interest," the core of which was U.S. security. But if self-preservation constituted the core of interest, there still had to be a dimension of interest that went beyond a concern for the self. While appreciating that the nation could not be expected to support a policy requiring the sacrifice of blood and treasure unless it was shown that vital interest, narrowly defined, demanded such sacrifice, Osgood also appreciated and emphasized that the nation would never remain committed in the postwar world unless it was persuaded that something other and greater than self-preservation was at stake. The history of the United States' principal foreign policy since World War II—containment—bears out this prescient analysis. The "order" side of containment (that is, the side responding to conventional security interest) has never evoked the enthusiasm that, on occasion, the "justice" side of containment has. The latter is the side responding to the vision we hold of our greater role in the world as the champion of freedom. And it has not done so despite the fact that over the years U.S. power has responded more to the former than to the latter.

When *Ideals and Self-Interest in America's Foreign Relations* first appeared, the nuclear age was still in its infancy. World War II had shown what conventional weapons might do when used with little or no restraint. Given the power of nuclear weapons, the need to have force strictly subordinated to the controlling requirements of political reason became all the more apparent. The experience of the Korean War dramatized this need and indicated its promise. In *Limited War* Osgood wrote what was at the time perhaps the most noteworthy analysis of that promise. Later, in *Force, Order, and Justice* he took up the same central question of the role of force as an instrument of conflict and order among states and placed it in broad historical perspective. *Force, Order, and Justice* began and ended with the proposition that military power remained an indispensable instrument of conflict and order in international politics and that nuclear weapons had not rendered it obsolete by depriving this power of its age-old functions.⟩

The present book may be seen against the background of these earlier efforts. Since the end of World War II, the peace and security of the United States and its major allies have depended largely on the deterrent effect of nuclear weapons. Any weapon may, and generally does, have a deterrent effect. What is novel about nuclear weapons is not that they have this effect but that they do so to an extent previously unknown, and this because of the consequences expected to follow from their use. Nuclear deterrence is something new under the sun because of the scope and intensity of the expectations raised by strategies dependent on nuclear weapons. These expectations reflect the twin conviction that peace and security are largely dependent on the deterrent effect of nuclear weapons and that the use of nuclear weapons would very likely lead to self-defeating destruction on a scale heretofore unknown⟩

The nuclear dilemma is the expression of this twin conviction that has given a distinctive quality to the postwar U.S. approach to military strategy. The history of U.S. strategic thought since World War II is largely the history of the various reactions to this dilemma. In these pages, Professor Osgood has examined the principal responses made to the nuclear dilemma and has done so with the critical insight and understanding that marked all of his writing.

Robert W. Tucker

1

Military Strategy and Security
in the Nuclear Era

THE ROLE OF STRATEGIC THOUGHT

In the period since World War II, the United States has encountered moral and strategic issues concerning the management of force in peacetime that are unique in its historical experience and novel in the history of international politics. At the core of these issues lies a dilemma—namely, the moral (as well as ethical) and strategic predicament of being unable to pursue one course of action without incurring the disadvantages of another.[1] It arises from the dependence of military security on nuclear weapons. This nuclear dilemma lurks in the background of every major military strategic choice and suffuses all the major strategic debates. The history of U.S. strategic thought can largely be comprehended as the story of how Americans have tried to cope with this dilemma by rejecting, abolishing, or mitigating it. This story not only illuminates the distinctive qualities of the U.S. approach to military strategy in the cold war, in all its ethical as well as expediential dimensions; it also tells us much about the moral and strategic issues of nuclear weapons that confront the whole world.

The nuclear dilemma is simply an expression of the momentous fact that the security and peace of the United States and its major allies depend heavily on the deterrent effect of nuclear weapons, and on the fact that this deterrent, if used, would very probably lead to self-defeating destruction and, possibly, an ecological catastrophe for much of civilization.

This dilemma plays a distinctively large role in U.S. strategic thought for several reasons.

1. The U.S. has the principal responsibility in the Western security community (including Japan) for deterring and constraining Soviet aggression overseas as well as against itself, and it controls the preponderant nuclear strength relevant to this end. This responsibility raises moral and expediential issues about the use of nuclear weapons against conventional aggression—issues of credibility and proportionality—that are particularly difficult to resolve and fraught with controversy.

2. These issues, though integrally related to highly technical military facts and judgments, are also fundamentally matters of political and psychological judgment—the natural province of social scientists rather than of the military profession.

3. The institutionalized U.S. tradition of challenging authority—especially military authority—gives civilian strategists a uniquely significant role in formulating and influencing policies concerning the use of armed force.

4. Because ethical principles and moral sensitivities have always played a central role in the nation's approach toward the use of force, as in the conduct of foreign policy in general, U.S. strategists have a special role to play in rationalizing and systematizing concepts of military security in terms of transcendent principles.

5. Strategies of deterrence are the principal means of supporting U.S. commitments through containment short of war. Strategies for the limitation of force promise to implement containment at a tolerable cost if force must be used. But because containment and the limitation of force (translated into strategic doctrine) rely on force to make force tolerable, they grate against the historic American aversion to managing and manipulating force, as opposed to renouncing it or unleashing it for victory. This tension stimulates doctrinal controversy and calls for an intellectual effort to resolve that controversy, an effort that civilian strategists have been well placed to undertake.

For these reasons, U.S. strategic thought has played the multifaceted role of rationalization, justification, criticism, and advocacy with respect to issues raised by the nuclear dilemma. This role is comparable to that played by political scientists, historians, economists, and other intellectuals with respect to other kinds of foreign policy issues raised by the novel experience of managing power on a global scale in peacetime. U.S. strategists are the intermediaries between the esoteric science and art of developing and using armed force on the one hand and the familiar challenge of reconciling power and purpose in pursuit of the national interest abroad on the other. In this role they have been notably influential. At the same time, their role has increasingly spread out among scientists, journalists, theologians, politicians, and other groups as the nuclear dilemma has increasingly impinged on the mind and conscience of a broader public.

Of course, U.S. operational strategy is the product of many factors—budgetary, bureaucratic, political, and technological—other than strategic thought. Yet strategic thought has been far more than a rationalization of the net result of these other factors. It has exerted a major influence in shaping operational strategy, particularly because the professional military has constantly looked to changing theories of civilian strategists, who go in and out of office, for intellectual support in interservice controversies and in the competition for defense funds. The relationship of strategic thought to force structures, targeting plans, procurement policies, and the like is seldom direct or logical. Yet military strategy, like economic theory, stands out as one of those few fields of intellectual inquiry that have had a pervasive influence on the policies and actions of the U.S. government.

The fact that a nuclear dilemma of profound moral significance lies at the core of U.S. strategic thought does not mean that strategists, in general, have been moral philosophers or even that they have been intensely or systematically concerned with the moral justification of their views. Most of them have been preoccupied with the practical or expediential aspects of the nuclear dilemma. Nevertheless, in the dominant strains of strategic thought, moral—especially humanitarian—concerns have been inextricably mixed with expediential reasoning; but such concerns have not been expressed merely for the purpose of rationalizing expediency or for the sake of argument. Indeed, strategic reasoning must play a large part in moral reasoning because it is so central to the link between intentions and consequences. Regardless of whether it is explicitly conscious of the moral dimension of military strategy, U.S. strategic thought impinges on all the moral issues raised by the nuclear dilemma. Therefore, an analytical survey of this body of thought should be an exercise of moral inquiry as well as one of descriptive generalization.

APPROACHES TO MORAL REASONING

A moral inquiry concerning the nuclear dilemma must come to grips with the fact that nuclear deterrence inevitably incurs a serious moral cost, whether or not the cost is a reasonable price to pay for its benefits. The moral cost arises from the inordinate human destructive potential of nuclear weapons, the implicit or explicit intention to use the nuclear weapons that deterrence presupposes, the possibility that deterrence may fail, and the great and incalculable risk that any use of nuclear weapons will escalate beyond a level of civil destruction proportionate to reasonable political gain.

Moral reasoning, however, can reach quite different conclusions about the policy implications of the moral cost of deterrence in any particular situation. Philosophers and theologians have no special claim to wisdom in this matter, since so much of moral judgment depends on assumptions about material, psychological, and political factors that bear upon hypothetical contingencies. But, by the same token, neither are scientists, social scientists, or even strategists entitled to such a claim.

To cope with the nuclear dilemma, moral reasoning must first relate the overt use of force to deterrence. Military deterrence—the dissuasion of adversaries from taking a hostile action by convincing them that this will incur an unacceptable risk of a military counteraction that will prevent their anticipated gain or make it too costly—presupposes a willingness to use force, no matter how unlikely or unwanted one regards this contingency. The most comprehensive and time-honored moral guidance for the resort to and overt use of force is found in the doctrine of just war. Because the actual employment of armed force is implicit in the threat or prospect of force, the doctrine of just war must be part of a doctrine of just deterrence.

These two objects of moral concern—deterring aggression and supporting deterrence with force—converge, but they are not identical. The principles of just cause—the exhaustion of peaceful alternatives, authoritative political control, means-to-ends effectiveness, proportionality of means to ends, and the avoidance of unnecessary civil damage—are notoriously ambiguous and thus difficult to apply. They are also notoriously susceptible to self-interested distortion. Nevertheless, one would be hard-pressed to improve upon them as moral guidelines for the overt use of force, including nuclear force.

But the doctrine of just war does not satisfy all the requirements of a doctrine of just deterrence. It pertains to only one of three interrelated objectives of a doctrine of just deterrence. The first two are *making deterrence as effective as possible* and *minimizing its dependence on nuclear weapons*. The third objective, to which the principles of just war apply, is *limiting and controlling the use of force* if deterrence should fail or be inapplicable. In the pursuit of these three objectives, prudential requirements converge with the moral imperatives of military strategy.

These three objectives should complement each other—but, pursued to their extremes, they may conflict with one another. Thus, the most destructive and least controllable threatened response to Soviet aggression (e.g., Herman Kahn's proverbial Doomsday Machine)[2] might be the most effective deterrent; if it were carried out, however, its physical and human destruction would automatically exceed the limits of a rational response to even the most extreme provocation. Similarly, a defensive posture that reduced NATO's dependence on a nuclear response to zero, assuming that effective conventional resistance capabilities were provided, would eliminate the immediate risk that resistance to aggression might be suicidal; but it might also weaken deterrence and therefore make war more likely. Strengthening NATO's conventional forces in order to avoid having to consider the early use of nuclear weapons might both strengthen nuclear deterrence and enhance the prospect of limiting and controlling a war for a reasonable negotiated purpose. It might strengthen deterrence by somewhat relieving allies of the terrible burden of resorting to nuclear war after failing to withstand a conventional blitzkrieg. It might facilitate the limitation and control of war by avoiding the terrible risk of nuclear escalation. But if the effort to strengthen conventional forces were interpreted principally as a sign of unwillingness to use nuclear weapons, and if the strengthened conventional forces were still incapable of preventing the Soviets from achieving a limited objective by conventional means, neither deterrence nor political control would be served. In reality, therefore, there are trade-offs in the advantages of pursuing one of the three objectives of just deterrence at the cost of another.

How one chooses to draw the optimal balance among these three objectives depends on judgments not only about their relative value but also about the feasibility, costs, and risks of implementing them. Thus, the extent to which one chooses to rely on the calculated limitation of military responses to aggression, whether conventional or nuclear, depends, among other things, on the feasibility of such limitation and the effects of the effort to implement this objective on arms competition and the defense budget.

Equally important, the balance one draws among these objectives will depend on one's risk-taking propensities and the assumption one makes about Soviet risk-taking propensities. More fundamentally still, the balance will depend on assumptions about the utility of force—whether overt, threatened, or implicit—in the nuclear age.

The history of U.S. strategic thought and the controversies related to it abundantly reflect the varying weights assigned to these three objectives. An analysis and synthesis of the principal competing patterns of strategic thought, therefore, will not only help explain this important aspect of postwar U.S. foreign policy and international politics but will also provide a data base, so to speak, for elaborating and refining the elements of a doctrine of just deterrence.

2

The Spectrum of Approaches
to the Nuclear Dilemma

The nuclear dilemma is so fundamental to postwar military strategy and so pervasive a factor in U.S. strategic thought that one can categorize this body of thought in terms of divergent approaches to coping with it. Three principal approaches stand out: *rejection, abolition,* and *mitigation.* Inasmuch as they correspond to basic approaches to the moral dimension of the dilemma, they constitute the basis for moral as well as expediential reasoning. The followers of *rejection* approach military strategy and arms control as though the nuclear dilemma does not exist. The proponents of *abolition* are convinced that the nuclear dilemma is so dangerous and immoral that it must be eliminated through disarmament. The advocates of *mitigation* believe that the dilemma is unavoidable but must and can be alleviated through strategy and arms control.

These categories of approach to the nuclear dilemma are not just ideal types. They are distillations of the views of real people. Not every strategic thinker fits neatly into one category. Some have shifted from one category to another. Others combine elements of one approach, qualified by another. But these three approaches do correspond to basic orientations, advocated or opposed by real people who have defined the core of the principal strategic controversies in the United States.

The proponents of mitigating the dilemma—the mitigators—are the principal source of elaboration and refinement of U.S. strategic concepts. They have exerted the principal influence on operational strategy. They also have been the principal generators and articulators of strategic controversies, which have turned upon two competing approaches to mitigation—let us call them *maximalist* and *minimalist* for lack of better words—which differ primarily in their respective emphases on the limitation and control of warfighting capabilities and on the unavoidable prospect of nuclear escalation leading to catastrophic damage. However, the rejectionists, as both operators and thinkers, have also exerted a major influence on strategic thought. They have helped provoke the mitigators to formulate their views and to apply them to operational strategy. And the abolitionists—who are more explicitly concerned with the moral than with the expediential dimension of the nuclear dilemma—have provided a continuing challenge to the theory and practice of mitigation. Indeed, this challenge has enlivened the strategic debate, pervaded official rhetoric, and occasionally sounded an echo in operational strategy, especially through the channel of arms control.

An examination of these three positions and how they have interacted in the controversies over the employment and restraint of force in the nuclear age will illuminate the entanglement of moral and expediential considerations in sufficient detail and complexity to enable us to return with enriched insights, in the final section of this study, to the challenge of outlining a doctrine of just deterrence.

THE REJECTIONISTS

The rejectionists reject the nuclear dilemma—whether deliberately or by indifference—in their approach to the management of force in the nuclear age. They see no moral or practical conflict between declaring and actually carrying out the strategy of deterrence, either because they are completely confident that the nuclear deterrent will work or because they have no practical or moral compunction about using nuclear weapons if deterrence fails. Among those who systematically and publicly articulate views about nuclear deterrence, there are now very few rejectionists—far fewer than during the first two decades of the cold war. But in those decades they left a permanent mark on U.S. strategic thought and military policies, if only by the opposition they aroused among mitigators and abolitionists. Moreover, their basic approach to deterrence seems to linger on, inexplicitly, in the programs and polemics of some of those who are strategic do-ers rather than thinkers.

The Warwinners

At the outset of the cold war and up to the Kennedy-McNamara administration, the most important rejectionists among the experts and professionals were to be found in the Strategic Air Command (SAC). SAC single-mindedly pursued a militarily offensive strategy of using nuclear weapons—and using them first and soon against a Soviet conventional attack in Western Europe—in order to defeat the Soviet Union by destroying its military-industrial assets and, as a "bonus" resulting from the urban location of these assets, by destroying millions of Soviet citizens as well.[3]

As the Soviet Union gained an intercontinental nuclear capability, it became the rejectionists' central objective not only to maintain the capacity to win a European war but also to deter a direct attack on the United States by maintaining the capacity to disarm the Soviets. As the number of nuclear bombs and the bombers and then missiles to deliver them increased, so did SAC's targets, which came to include various military or counterforce targets (principally, nuclear weapons) as well as countervalue targets (that is, concentrations of people and economic life). But SAC leaders, such as General Curtis LeMay and General Thomas Powers, convinced of the decisive offensive capabilities of air power, continued to reject any effort to alter war plans so as to spare cities or in any way limit the infliction of maximum destruction with maximum speed. This group of rejectionists might be called the *warwinners* because they believed that effective deterrence had to be based on obliterating the USSR's capacity to fight—no holds barred—in accordance with the most unrestricted methods of strategic bombing practiced in World War II.

The Finite Deterrers

In the late 1950s another kind of rejectionism emerged, based on an absolute commitment to deterrence rather than to military victory. It arose from an effort to combine the prevention of Soviet aggression with a deep aversion to war and the arms race. Its prescription was finite (or minimum) deterrence. Underlying the prescription was the conviction that the only feasible and moral kind of deterrence is mutual deterrence based on U.S. and Soviet possession of the minimum nuclear capabilities needed to inflict unacceptable civil damage by striking a finite number of the adversary's cities. The *finite deterrers*, impressed by the awesome explosive power of thermonuclear weapons and anxious to curb the arms race, believed that the best guarantee of peace at a reasonable cost lay in the "balance of terror" based on a parity and sufficiency of countervalue capabilities in the United States and USSR, pending the achievement of total disarmament. They opposed hedging against the incredibility or failure of deterrence with counterforce warfighting capabilities or strategies to limit and control force. Such strategies would stimulate the arms race and make war more likely by making nuclear weapons seem more usable and provoking either side to strike first because it feared being stuck. By placing all their faith in deterrence, they rejected—or at least circumvented—the moral dilemma inherent in the prospect of actually using the deterrent.

Finite deterrence, in the general sense of a nuclear strategy and based entirely on the assumption that the Soviets would be deterred from any major provocation (such as an all-out attack against Western Europe) because they feared overwhelming civil destruction in retaliation, was the popular view that prevailed into the 1960s. In its absolute sense, finite deterrence was never widespread among strategic thinkers. But the basic idea underlying finite deterrence—that parity of countervalue capabilities provides the best road to peace and disarmament—became a powerful force in the opposition to antiballistic missiles (ABMs) in the 1960s and in the support of the nuclear freeze movement in the 1980s. This idea became the favorite butt of criticism by the proponents of strategies of limited counterforce. As the Soviet capacity to inflict comparable retaliatory damage on the United States grew, it provided a great stimulus to the mitigators and a great boon to their influence.

In the latter half of the 1950s, this kind of rejectionism was briefly advocated by the U.S. Navy (in collaboration with the Army against the Air Force). Naval leaders regarded finite deterrence as conveniently suited to the submarine-launched Polaris missile's claim to a major strategic role; the Polaris would be cheaper and less vulnerable than strategic bombers. But their advocacy was suspect because in the congressional hearings of 1949, the Navy had opposed relying on B-36 bombers instead of aircraft carriers partly on the humanitarian grounds that a strategy of inflicting maximum civil destruction was immoral.

By the end of the 1950s, when the concept of mutual deterrence gained currency, the core of finite-deterrence rejectionism was made up of scientists and humanitarians who, paradoxically, were most articulately sensitive to the moral enormity of nuclear warfare. On the principle that the most effective deterrent to war is the most devastating and least avoidable form of retaliation, they opposed efforts to make retaliation rationally useful by limiting its damage. Any effort to limit and control an East-West war, they charged, was not only illusory but provocative, because it would obscure the inevitably catastrophic nature of such a war. Any effort to diminish the mutual vulnerability of national populations to nuclear obliteration would stimulate the arms race and destabilize the East-West military equilibrium.

Deterrence and Arms Control

Although these two groups of rejectionists diametrically opposed each other's military strategies, they joined in rejecting the moral and expediential implications of the nuclear dilemma that increasingly troubled abolitionists and mitigators. The fate of the two groups of rejectionists was played out principally in the course of two strategic episodes: (1) the Eisenhower-Dulles "New Look" strategy, which pledged the United States to rely on the deterrent power of the U.S. capacity for "massive retaliation" in order to avoid, and avoid preparing for, future Korean-type wars at places and by means of the adversary's choice, and (2) the ABM debate of the 1960s. The warwinners' perspective dominated the New Look. The spirit of finite deterrence infused the ABM debate and, with the achievement of the ABM Treaty, apparently won in the marketplace of strategic ideas and in specific defense policies. However, it was the mitigators and abolitionists who prevailed in the longer run, as consciousness of the inordinate costs of carrying out nuclear deterrence spread and deepened.

The Eisenhower-Dulles administration, in effect, endorsed warwinning rejectionism when it proclaimed and adopted a strategic formula for strengthened deterrence with budgetary retrenchment after the Korean War. In NSC 162/2 it authorized the Joint Chiefs of Staff (JCS) to act on the principle that nuclear weapons are like conventional weapons and should be used, and used first and soon, for the traditional military objective of defeating the enemy as quickly and thoroughly as possible. The Joint Chiefs and especially SAC interpreted their guidance for warplanning and warfighting accordingly.

On the other hand, President Dwight Eisenhower and Secretary of State John Foster Dulles, partly in response to domestic and foreign apprehensions, soon qualified their declaratory strategy by acknowledging the possibility of less-than-massive responses to aggression in some circumstances.[4] Secretary Dulles noted the value of ambiguity about the exact nature of a response to aggression when combined with clarity of commitment to respond in some way. In crises and local wars outside Europe (the only territories in which the application of the threat of massive retaliation was new), the declaratory threat was, in fact, confined to limited nuclear counterforce responses to blunt direct military attacks by China. In the one case in which this threat was used as a compellent (to end the Korean War), and in the two cases in which it was used as a deterrent (to save Dienbienphu and to prevent a Communist Chinese attack against Quemoy and Matsu), the evidence strongly suggests that Eisenhower and Dulles did not actually regard carrying out the threat as in the national interest, on either military or political grounds.[5]

These qualifications to an all-out warwinning strategy could be dismissed as rhetorical concessions to domestic and foreign opinion, with no general operational significance. More plausibly and significantly, however, they could be interpreted as the result of defense-budget austerity and the diplomacy of nuclear coercion (verging on bluff), both of which were running up against the realities of self-deterrence in the nuclear age. The disparity between strategic plans and their implementation was a manifestation of the inescapable ambivalence that future presidents and their foreign and defense officers would feel even more intensely when confronting the contradiction between the utility—indeed, the necessity—of nuclear weapons for deterrence and the absurdity of actually using the full destructive potential of nuclear weapons to achieve any reasonable political objective. The record of Eisenhower's private statements about nuclear weapons and plans is full of such contradictions as this, marked by his insistence, on the one hand, that the United States plan to use its most powerful weapons to avoid defeat at home or abroad and by his dire warnings, on the other hand, that any nuclear war would be an unimaginable and self-defeating disaster for the United States and humankind.[6]

To be sure, Eisenhower's reservations about the use of nuclear weapons were stated with respect to local conflicts outside Europe. As he assumed that any Soviet aggression within Europe would quickly lead to total war, the issue of nonnuclear or limited nuclear war did not arise there. It took the growing capacity of the USSR to devastate the United States—most conspicuously in the 1960s and 1970s—to impress upon Eisenhower's successors the necessity of mitigating NATO's nuclear dilemma by strengthening nonnuclear responses to aggression. Eisenhower's concern was to redress Soviet superiority in conventional forces with tactical nuclear weapons, in accordance with NATO's strategic document MC 14/2. These weapons were regarded as an adjunct to a general nuclear warfighting capability, not as an instrument of limited war. Nevertheless, Eisenhower was impelled to articulate the resulting dilemma while rejecting its strategic consequences. While proclaiming the United States' unwillingness—indeed, inability—to fight a war of local resistance, and while reiterating his conviction that any war in Europe would be a thermonuclear war, he also declared on numerous occasions that such a war would be "self-defeating" and would bring about "the destruction of civilization as we know it."[7]

That this ambivalence had so little impact on official strategic doctrine and none at all on military plans and programs in Eisenhower's administration can be explained by the fact that the nation as a whole still enjoyed, or believed that it enjoyed, the kind of nuclear superiority that might halt a major Soviet aggression and decisively win a general war. Consistent with this faith in superiority was the fact that even many of those mitigators who in the mid-1950s had deplored the United States' growing dependence on a nuclear deterrent that would be irrational and immoral to carry out believed that massive retaliation was a credible threat to deter an attack against Western Europe.[8]

Before the end of the 1950s, however, the Eisenhower-Dulles administration's operational rejection of the nuclear dilemma elicited a strong revulsion among civilian and U.S. Army strategists. The reaction against massive retaliation and the concomitant movement toward the discriminating use of force, led by the mitigators at the RAND Corporation, were decisive blows to warwinning rejectionism—the more so when President John Kennedy embraced the mitigators' views and brought many of the proponents of mitigation into the government. The reaction against the warwinners left the propogation of the rejectionist approach to the advocates of finite deterrence, who combined the same indifference to the nuclear dilemma with a much more intense defense-budget austerity and an absolute confidence that only a few nuclear weapons would deter major Soviet aggressions. But the resurgent fear of the Soviet threat in the final years of Eisenhower's presidency spelled an end to defense austerity. President Eisenhower's difficulty in holding the line on defense expenditures (under assault by the Sputnik alarm, the missile-gap crisis, and the collapse of the Spirit of Geneva) helped move the proponents of absolute and finite deterrence to look to arms control instead of defense policy as the medium in which to express their strategic convictions.

Arms control became a major battle ground of strategic ideas in the 1960s. At the center of this phenomenon was the controversy over antiballistic missiles. As the ABM debate gathered force in the 1960s, many of the warwinning rejectionists—after they overcame their initial aversion to defensive, as opposed to offensive, weapons and tactics—joined the maximalist mitigators in becoming staunch advocates of strategic defense weapons as a means of limiting damage to the national population and, later, as a means of protecting ICBMs against a major Soviet attack, or at least protecting people against a lesser Chinese attack.

The proponents of finite deterrence, however, lined up solidly against ABMs. They argued that ABMs could not actually protect cities against offensive missiles, as the offense would always have an intrinsic advantage. But they also argued that the deployment of ABMs would encourage the illusion of being able to protect national populations, and that this illusion would both embolden the United States to believe that it could wage nuclear war with impunity and provoke the USSR to strike preventively or preemptively in order to protect its population against a U.S. first strike, shielded by ABMs against retaliatory damage. Above all, these rejectionists were opposed to ABMs on the grounds that their deployment would stimulate a fruitless and dangerous arms race, which could be avoided simply by keeping a minimum quantity of U.S. retaliatory forces invulnerable (i.e., by hardening bases, concealing weapons at sea, and other means).

In these arguments, but from a different strategic perspective, which did not totally reject counterforce warfighting capabilities, the advocates of finite deterrence were joined by the minimalist mitigators, who, with Secretary of Defense Robert S. McNamara in the lead, contrived the formula for aborting the ABM program in the ABM Treaty. Designed to stabilize the strategic offensive balance at parity of second-strike capabilities to inflict "assured destruction," the ABM Treaty codified the view (which was anathema to maximalist mitigators) that the best way to curb the costs and dangers of the nuclear arms race was to keep people as hostages to the threat of obliteration while making the weapons to kill them invulnerable. Thus, it was altogether logical that the minimalists, like the proponents of finite deterrence, should become the most unqualified supporters of the strategy maximalists condemned as MAD (mutual assured destruction) when ABMs threatened to replace the reliance of strategic deterrence on nuclear retaliation with reliance on a damage-limiting warfighting strategy.

Until the mid-1970s the concept of MAD—whether viewed as an unqualified objective or as an unavoidable necessity— prevailed in the intellectual rationalization and articulation of strategy and arms control. But the significance of MAD was importantly qualified by the fact that throughout the 1960s the United States enjoyed a clear-cut superiority in nuclear striking power and, therefore, in the capacity to fight a damage-limiting counterforce war if nuclear deterrence failed. Correspondingly, the loss of the United States' strategic superiority since the mid-1960s has generated growing dissatisfaction with reliance on MAD. The momentous growth of Soviet nuclear capabilities has undermined support for both kinds of rejectionist views. It has had this effect not so much because of a declining faith in nuclear deterrence, and certainly not because of a heightened fear of Soviet attack, but primarily because of the political, intellectual, and moral strain of maintaining the credibility and acceptability of an early nuclear first-use strategy in NATO Europe as the Soviet capacity to devastate the United States as well as Western Europe has steadily increased. In addition, the increased accuracy and lower yields of nuclear weapons, the improvements in command, control, communication, and intelligence systems (C^3I), and the prospect that conventional weapons may replace some functions of counterforce nuclear weapons have raised hopes, championed by the maximalist mitigators, that deterrence can be based on more discriminating weapons that inflict less collateral damage. This new military technology, in the minds of its most ardent promoters, promises to relieve deterrence of its excessive dependence on holding people hostage to MAD.

The growing dissatisfaction with MAD has meant that a warwinning, as opposed to a flexible and controlled warfighting strategy, has fallen into general disrepute; a strategy of finite deterrence is commonly condemned by experts; and MAD has become a familiar acronym of opprobrium. However, since old strategic ideas never quite die but always seem to return in a new form, it may be premature to declare the complete demise of rejectionism. Warwinning rejectionism may live on in the operational plans and propensities of some members of the military, as a response to the ingrained professional axiom that we must defeat the enemy before the enemy defeats us. It may survive in spirit, at least, in the doctrines of some of the more militant warfighting strategists, who think it essential to be able to "prevail" in a nuclear war.

Finite deterrence survives in spirit as the philosophical core of opposition to counterforce and damage-limiting strategies. It is the strategic doctrine of antimilitary and pacifist groups, insofar as they feel the need of one. Finite deterrence might even experience a revival among systematic strategic thinkers if schemes for deep nuclear reductions (with or without the help of conventional ballistic missile defense [BMD] weapons) should gain credence, as, in that instance, the most efficient use of a small number of penetrating weapons might seem to be targeting cities in an intrawar bargaining strategy. Nevertheless, the rejectionists, who ascended in an early period of scarce and inaccurate nuclear striking power combined with U.S. nuclear superiority, most likely have permanently subsided in influence as compared with the abolitionists and mitigators. It could hardly be otherwise, given the powerful forces that have converged to accentuate the nuclear dilemma.

The continuing adverse shift in the East-West military balance and the growing fear that the enhanced usability of nuclear weapons might actually lead to their use—in combination with the chastening experience of a failed limited war in Vietnam and the subsequent disillusionment with détente in the 1970s— have challenged the champions of flexible and controlled response, just as the mitigators challenged and largely replaced the rejectionists. Accordingly, the abolitionists have once again, as at the onset of the nuclear age, become major contenders in the marketplace of security ideas. The major expediential and moral controversies about military strategy are now channeled into a debate between abolitionists and mitigators. But the same factors that have energized the abolitionists have, in fact, stimulated a lively debate between the minimalist and maximalist mitigators.

The latter debate has been conducted in terms of many of the issue categories that pitted the maximalist mitigators against the minimum deterrence rejectionists. The maximalists accuse the minimalists of being covert adherents of MAD. The minimalists accuse the maximalists of being virtual adherents of a nuclear warwinning strategy. But in both cases the terms of the debate revolve around the issue of how to cope with the nuclear dilemma, not how to reject or abolish it. It is this debate, not the one precipitated by the abolitionists, that will affect actual policies and programs in defense and arms control, even though these policies and programs are increasingly presented to domestic and world opinion in the rhetoric of abolition.

THE ABOLITIONISTS

In the beginning of the cold war there were the abolitionists. They were members of the early peace and antinuclear movement, which was particularly strong in England, where it was represented by the flourishing Campaign for Nuclear Disarmament. Their stronghold was among U.S. scientists, many of whom had worked on the atomic bomb and were horrified by the terrible power they had released.[9] The scientists were joined by left-wing journalists, humanitarians, and pacifists, who found in this power a confirmation of their convictions about the evil of force.

The abolitionists were sure that any East-West war would be a nuclear war and that a nuclear war would reduce both sides and, possibly, the world to radiated rubble, as portrayed in Nevil Shute's novel *On the Beach*.[10] But they had no confidence that this prospect would keep the peace through nuclear deterrence. They viewed arms control, at best, as a step toward total disarmament and, at worst, as a device to make militarism and the arms race more acceptable. Even before the Soviets were able to build nuclear bombers that could reach the United States and return, the abolitionists found the thought of using or planning to use nuclear weapons morally abhorrent. They believed that the Soviet acquisition of nuclear weapons would mark not a bilateral nuclear stalemate but the beginning of a rapid proliferation of such weapons to other countries throughout the world, which would lead to unbearable insecurity and, eventually, a catastrophic global war.

Consequently, the abolitionists were preoccupied with the question of how to eliminate the nuclear danger at its presumed source, the weapons themselves—not with the issue of how to mitigate the nuclear dilemma. This danger, in their view, arose from the erroneous belief that nuclear weapons might be useful, whether for deterrence or for war. The solution, therefore, was not merely to abolish nuclear weapons but to abolish the whole "war system." To abolitionists this was a system marked by an obsolete historical habit of regarding force—now including nuclear weapons—as an instrument of policy.

After the U.S. and Soviet hydrogen bomb tests in the 1950s and the thawing of the cold war in the 1960s, it became harder to believe that nuclear weapons would inevitably be used. It became easier to believe that nuclear weapons, rather than leading to Armageddon, might be the basis of mutal deterrence, precisely because governments also regarded them as, if not uniquely abhorrent, at least uniquely terrifying. But the popular recognition of the deterrent effect of nuclear armaments scarcely moderated the abolitionists' absolute abhorrence of nuclear weapons. Deterrence, in their view, would only delay the eventual catastrophe that the arms race would surely produce. Therefore, the only salvation lay in "banning the bomb," "delegitimizing" nuclear weapons, eliminating them through disarmament, eradicating the social and economic bases of the war system, or establishing some form of world government— "One World or None," in the words of the slogan borrowed from a popular pamphlet on the atomic danger.[11] The mounting fear of nuclear fallout from tests, following the surprising

contamination of the Japanese fishing boat *Lucky Dragon* in
March 1954 and culminating in the nuclear test ban debate
of the 1960s, greatly accentuated the atmosphere of popular
nuclear anxieties within which abolitionism thrived. But with
the fading of hopes for exorcising the nuclear menace through
campaigns and demonstrations, or for circumventing it through
world government, many abolitionists turned to disarmament
as the last best hope for mankind.

The abolitionists reached the peak of their influence on
military and foreign policy with the Baruch Plan, which the
United States government presented as the solution to the
nuclear problem in 1946. The Baruch Plan prescribed the
abolition of nuclear weapons by putting nuclear materials under
international ownership and eliminating the Security Council's
veto on violations of the treaty. The Soviets, of course, could
not accept an agreement that would freeze the U.S. advantage
in nuclear know-how, but neither side could have accepted the
international ownership *and* no-veto provisions. Moreover, the
abolition of nuclear weapons ran directly contrary to U.S.
military strategy, which made nuclear weapons indispensable
in order to compensate for conventional inferiority in Europe.
But the Baruch Plan was very popular. Because Moscow rejected
it, the plan was a gratifying weapon of the cold war as well
as an uplifting claim to the moral high ground.

Repeated Soviet rejections of the plan and U.S. dominance
of Security Council voting relieved the United States of the
need to face up to the consequences of abolitionism. By the
mid-1950s, however, the combination of stalemated negotiations, artful Soviet concessions that raised the awkward possibility of serious negotiations, and the spread of East-West
hostility led to the demise of the Baruch Plan. After 1957 the
emergence of the nuclear test ban issue largely replaced disarmament as the battlefield of struggle for the moral high
ground. The vision of disarmament lingered on in the propaganda of general and complete disarmament (GCD), which
the Soviets tried to exploit as their functional equivalent of
the Baruch Plan; but in the 1960s the abolitionists turned to
the more diffuse agenda of the peace movement and to the
organized opposition to ABMs as the principal media for

influencing public policy. By the late 1950s the intellectual balance of power was shifting from disarmament toward arms control, which civilian strategists from the growing school of mitigators formulated as the diplomatic counterpart of strategies for the discriminating use of force.

In the 1960s and through most of the 1970s, the abolitionists could find public influence only by aligning themselves with the antimilitary and anti-Vietnam causes, in which disaffected mitigators took the lead. In both its polemical and theoretical forms, abolitionism receded into the background of the sometimes esoteric but increasingly lively debate of the late 1950s and early 1960s about defense policy and arms control—a debate dominated by the mitigators. By the end of the 1970s, however, other developments were beginning to excite popular anxieties about nuclear weapons: the collapse of the U.S.-Soviet détente, the abortion of SALT II, the revival of the peace movement in European popular opposition to deployments of intermediate-range nuclear forces (INF), scientific elaboration of the dangers of "nuclear winter," and expert revelations of the deficiencies of positive command and control over nuclear weapons. These developments provided the abolitionists with an invigorated cause. But this time, the cause of abolition was expressed in more explicitly moral, if no less apocalyptic, terms. Its major policy focus was the nuclear freeze movement of the early 1980s.[12] Its major institutional allies were the American Catholic theologians, who, in alignment with liberal scientists, launched a well-orchestrated attack against nuclear deterrence and limited nuclear options. In theory, the ultimate ally of the abolitionists of the 1980s could well have been President Reagan, who, in his formulation of the strategic defense initiative (SDI) in March 1983, proclaimed a military technology and strategy intended to make nuclear weapons "impotent and obsolete." In practice, however, SDI was their enemy, since it proposed to reach the abolitionist goal by the counterforce route favored by maximalist mitigators.

We shall return to this drama after examining mitigation and the debate between minimalist and maximalist mitigators. This debate dominated the strategic and arms control controversies of the late 1970s, just as it had dominated the earlier

ABM debate. For it was this debate that most clearly illuminated the issues posed by the nuclear dilemma, which both the moral abolitionists and the Reagan abolitionists hoped to overcome.

THE MITIGATORS

Minimalists and Maximalists

The mitigators believe not only that the United States confronts a nuclear dilemma, with an expediential and moral dimension, but also that we must make the best of this dilemma. In other words, we must mitigate the dangers of deterrence in the nuclear age even while we capitalize on its advantages, unless, some would add, an equally effective and stable system of deterrence that is not dependent on nuclear force can be found as a substitute. To mitigate the dangers—principally, the challenge to the credibility of extended deterrence (nuclear first-use in Europe) and the risk that any use of nuclear weapons will escalate beyond rational control—the mitigators advocate reducing reliance on nuclear responses to aggression, principally by strengthening conventional denial capabilities in NATO, developing effective limited-force options, and stabilizing the arms competition and the military balance through arms control.

Arms control, in the mitigators' view, should aim above all toward the preservation of a stable and predictable military equilibrium that would be less prone to war in crises; it should also complement military security by curbing the weapons most threatening to the equilibrium. The overriding standard of achievement should be the strengthening of mutual deterrence. Toward that end, the USSR would, at the least, have to be denied a rationally usable first-strike capability; but in the eyes of the minimalists, in particular; *both* sides would have to be denied a first-strike capability, lest Soviet fear of a first strike provoke a preemptive attack. Preventing first-strike capabilities, in this view, depends preeminently on the assurance of sufficient invulnerable retaliatory capabilities, unless or until (some maximalists would add) the weapons to defend national populations against nuclear strikes have enabled both sides to base deterrence on mutual assured survival instead of mutual assured destruction.

The minimalist and maximalist mitigators[13] share more views than they disagree upon. Their differences with the rejectionists and the abolitionists are much greater and more distinct than those among themselves. But their own differences, although largely matters of degree and emphasis, are the most important substantively as well as in terms of their role in the history of strategic controversies. These differences—although they are points on a spectrum of ideas, and some individual strategists combine elements of both categories—can be divided into the maximalist and minimalist strategic approaches to mitigating the adversities of nuclear deterrence.[14]

The principal difference between maximalists and minimalists is that the former group, distrusting the long-run reliability of basing deterrence on perceptions of the national will and resolve to run risks of mutual suicide, strives to make the correspondence between the deterrence threat and the rational utility of carrying it out as close as possible. The maximalists prefer not to leave deterrence to fallible calculations of national will and resolve. For them, the only credible and safe deterrent is one that the nation would be willing to carry out if deterrence failed. The minimalists, by contrast, have more confidence that nuclear deterrence will work even if it is not useful to carry out; at the same time, they have less confidence that nuclear force can be limited and controlled so as to make it rationally useful. Therefore, they put greater emphasis on the psychological and political elements of deterrence—especially the balance of interests, intentions, and resolve; the factor of uncertainty in the potential aggressor's mind; and the possibility of affecting that aggressor's behavior by demonstrating and bargaining with limited force, at least at the lower levels of violence. The minimalists rely less than the maximalists on the pursuit of effective warfighting capabilities. In other words, the maximalists try to avoid or minimize the element of bluff in deterrence, whereas the minimalists tend to believe that in East-West deterrence a large gap between the threat and the rationality or will of actually carrying it out is intrinsic to the nuclear age and, moreover, that it is a dangerous and costly illusion to try to close the gap beyond a certain minimal point.

These divergent strategic outlooks pertain not only to different approaches to deterrence but also to different approaches to the use of force if deterrence fails. Maximalists stress the imperative of protecting the national population from nuclear damage by military and nonmilitary (civil defense) means, not only for humanitarian reasons but also for the sake of post-attack national survival and a favorable outcome of the war. They believe that some kind of reciprocal war limitation, even in strategic nuclear exchanges—preferably based on controlled counterforce strikes—is indispensable to interwar deterrence and rational war termination. Minimalists are more skeptical of the feasibility of limiting nuclear exchanges and protecting the national population in a strategic war, place relatively more value on preventing nuclear war than on being prepared to fight it, are concerned that an emphasis on warfighting will be at the expense of deterrence, and put more faith in the threat of graduated punitive action than in escalating force-attrition as a means of intrawar deterrence and war termination.

Integrally related to these divergent outlooks is the minimalists' emphasis on moderating the arms competition (a stance consistent with minimum security requirements) and the maximalists' disposition to call for as great an arms effort, quantitatively and qualitatively, as is needed and as the political traffic will bear in order to back deterrence with effective force. Concomitantly, the maximalists have greater confidence than the minimalists in the capacity of technology to close the gap between deterrent threat and capability, and less confidence that arms agreements can compensate for warfighting capabilities as an instrument of national security.

Logically related to these differences is the maximalists' pessimistic and the minimalists' more optimistic assumption about both the likelihood and the intensity of the Soviet military threat that is to be deterred. The maximalists tend to take Soviet capabilities as the operational guide to Soviet intentions. The minimalists see no close correspondence between capabilities and intention and tend to discount Soviet risk-taking propensities. It follows that the maximalists urge the United

States to operate on the premise that even marginal Soviet advantages in warfighting capabilities pose a danger of aggression, or in any case a danger of intimidation, that must be offset. In contrast, the minimalists believe that, given the simple existence of redundant nuclear destructive potential on both sides and the great cautiousness of the Soviet Union in avoiding a direct military encounter with the United States, the threat of aggression and intimidation can be offset within relatively wide disparities of warfighting capabilities. For this reason the maximalists see the East-West military balance as more "delicate" (in Albert Wohlstetter's description)—that is, more prone to destabilization—than the minimalists. The minimalists are inclined to see the balance as relatively robust so long as the United States does not overreact to marginal gains and anticipated "gaps" and thereby create a self-fulfilling prophecy.

Neither kind of mitigator approaches the strategic issues of deterrence primarily from a moral or ethical standpoint. The origins of mitigation lie in (1) the economist's approach to making rational choices (in this case, among weapons systems and strategies for using them) in order to find the optimal way to support a hierarchy of values (in this case, the nation's security objectives) and (2) the approach of the political scientist and historian from the postwar realist school, which is wedded to the Clausewitzian view that force must be limited and controlled in order to serve political ends, lest war become indiscriminate violence. The major articulators of ethical concerns about issues of strategy and arms control have been scientists and clergy, who are not generally sympathetic to mitigation theory and policies. Nonetheless, the mitigators' opposition to rejectionism reflects a strong revulsion against the undiscriminating use of force and a strong disposition to save lives and limit civil damage—a stance as much humanitarian as expediential. Moreover, ethical concerns have explicitly played a prominent role in the controversies between minimalists and maximalists, especially in the controversy that is popularly conceived as turning upon a choice between the strategies of MAD and limited counterforce.

In facing the ethical dimension of the nuclear dilemma directly, the maximalists tend to emphasize the inordinate moral cost of basing deterrence on the mutual vulnerability of national populations to obliteration, which they condemn as a particularly pernicious form of holding civilian hostages; they also stress the unacceptable moral risk of relying on chance, uncertainty, and relative resolve instead of on effective warfighting strength to support deterrence. The minimalists, on the other hand, emphasize the impracticability of mitigating (and the counterproductivity of trying to mitigate) the moral cost of the nuclear dilemma by developing a completely rational and effective warfighting capability. They seek to absolve themselves of the onus of deliberately basing deterrence on a potentially catastrophic response to aggression by arguing that the deterrent effect of capabilities for mutual assured destruction is "existential"; in other words, they believe that it is intrinsic to the superpowers' possession of immense nuclear power and the incalculable possibility that this power will be used, no matter what the precise operational strategies and plans for using it may be.[15]

Variations on Minimalist/Maximalist Thought

When the history of mitigation is considered, about a dozen economists, mathematicians, and political scientists stand out for both their intellectual contribution to and their influence on official military strategy, defense policies, and arms control. In addition, somewhat less than a dozen academics have indirectly exerted an important (but difficult to evaluate) influence on strategy and arms control through their contributions to the marketplace of ideas from which policymakers have drawn insights and intellectual reinforcement. The great majority of all these mitigators can be arranged on one side or the other of the maximalist/minimalist spectrum. A few must be placed in the middle. Fewer still have oscillated between one side or the other, or are difficult to classify for other reasons. The cases that defy simple classification tell us more than the less ambiguous cases about the intrinsic difficulties of pursuing a consistently rational and coherent position on mitigating the nuclear dilemma. Of those prominent mitigators whose place on the spectrum is ambiguous or oscillating, three are illustrative: Bernard Brodie, Donald Brennan, and Thomas Schelling.

In the first and seminal scholarly effort to examine the implications of nuclear weapons for military strategy and international politics—*The Absolute Weapon* (1946)—Bernard Brodie wrote two chapters in which he seemed to construct the foundation for a strategy of minimum countercity deterrence vis-à-vis the prospective of a nuclear Soviet Union in the next ten or twenty years. Starting with the assumption that the scarcity of fissionable materials meant that the primary targets of the atomic bomb would be cities, he reasoned that when both the United States and the USSR had enough bombs to destroy each other, additional bombs would lose their significance. He then reached the conclusion that the mutual fear of retaliation, based on invulnerable bombers and rockets located away from cities, would deter a surprise attack because no attack could gain anything worth the price of the resulting national destruction. In the most widely quoted statement in strategic literature—the favorite of those who derogate the rationality or morality of flexible and controlled nuclear strikes—Brodie asserted, "Thus far the chief purpose of our military establishment has been to win wars. From now on its chief purpose must be to avert them. It can have almost no other useful purpose."[16] Some have interpreted this view as an argument for finite deterrence or, at least, extreme minimalism, but Brodie was never content with any such absolute policy prescription. In his writings the question is always one of how to balance the threat of nuclear escalation and destruction with warfighting capabilities and how to weigh the prospect of limiting and controlling conventional or nuclear force against the prospect that force will get out of control and be self-defeating.

In 1951, when he learned of the many times greater explosive power of the thermonuclear bomb, Brodie decided that the means of destruction had become too extreme and efficient to make retaliation against cities rational. Drawing upon an insight he had reached as early as 1948, he now reasoned that Clausewitz's principle—that war should be an extension of politics by other means—dictated that the essence of nuclear strategy must be to avoid striking cities but also to use the threat of nuclear strikes to hold cities hostage while seeking to end the war on terms short of total surrender or destruction.[17] Implicit in this reasoning were the rudiments of a strategy of limited nuclear options.

Brodie also applied the strategy of limited nuclear options to the defense of Western Europe, where he saw the use of nuclear weapons against military targets as the only way to offset Soviet conventional superiority. But in the 1950s he decided that battlefield nuclear weapons were too prone to inflicting indiscriminate civil damage to make a NATO strategy of limited nuclear war feasible or useful. Like everyone else at RAND, he was a critic of the Eisenhower-Dulles emphasis on massive retaliation, but he also pointed out the limited utility and feasibility of the maximalist alternatives.[18] In the 1960s, nevertheless, he argued against the advocates of drawing a clear line—a "firebreak"—between the use of conventional and nuclear weapons in order to minimize the risk of nuclear war. Instead, he argued in favor of a strategy of minimum conventional resistance plus nuclear escalation, on the grounds of both alliance cohesion and deterrence.[19]

Throughout, Brodie was in every sense a mitigator looking for ways to make nuclear weapons serve rational political ends, but his oscillations on the maximalist/minimalist spectrum demonstrated the intrinsic difficulty of achieving this purpose. They also reflected the impact of changes in military technology with regard to expediential and moral considerations of strategy, as well as the decisive effect on strategic judgments with respect to the role of force in international politics.

In the 1950s Donald Brennan, a mathematician closely associated with the most widely known maximalist of the time, Herman Kahn, at the Hudson Institute, was a leader in developing the minimalist approach to arms control as a means of limiting the risk of nuclear war and enhancing national security. In the famous fall 1960 issue of *Daedalus* magazine (and in a book incorporating this issue with additional articles, published in 1961),[20] Brennan hoped to demonstrate, in response to those who criticized arms control as an evil means of perpetuating the arms race, the intellectual and moral superiority of arms limitation as compared to the classic concept of comprehensive disarmament. In his chapter "Setting and Goals of Arms Control," he cautiously, and with qualifications, set forth the long-term case in favor of comprehensive arms limitation, based on approximate equality of U.S. and Soviet second-strike capabilities, as a means of reducing the risk of war and avoiding an arms race that would increase destructive capabilities without enhancing security—the favorite formula of the minimalists.

In dealing with the issue of deterring major conventional attack with a nuclear first-use strategy—whether strategic or tactical—Brennan took the position that this kind of extended deterrence was too costly, insufficiently credible, and ineffective in protecting the object of aggression. Instead, he believed that the NATO countries should build an effective conventional resistance force. But in the early 1960s he became a critic of what he regarded as an overemphasis in the strategic community on conventional capabilities and an unwarranted depreciation of the value of tactical nuclear weapons. Like Brodie, he was sympathetic to the European approach to extended deterrence.[21]

By 1964, however, Brennan's skepticism about the effectiveness of nuclear deterrence against anything but a nuclear attack had led him to commit his efforts to the maximalists' strategic solution with respect to disciplining the nuclear dilemma: the use of ABMs to defend people instead of making them hostage to nuclear annihilation. He then became one of the most vociferous critics of MAD (an acronym he is said to have invented), ridiculing and condemning as immoral and irrational the minimalist anti-ABM position that killing rather than protecting people is the safest, soundest deterrent. Again, as in the case of Brodie, there was an underlying consistency in the objectives and values Brennan was trying to reconcile within the mitigationist orientation; but technological changes and reaction to the twists and turns of public controversy over weapons led him to shift from a largely minimalist approach to a maximalist one.

Thomas Schelling, an economist with experience in trade negotiation, did not shift on the spectrum of mitigation—but, then, he is more difficult than most strategic thinkers to place on this spectrum. The reason is that he shared the maximalists' confidence in the feasibility of a limited, flexible, and controlled warfighting capability—nuclear as well as conventional—that would make a strategy of deterrence rationally useful to carry out, and he believed in the necessity of intrawar deterrence to terminate a war within limits of destruction that would keep the costs of war within bounds rationally related to political ends. At the same time, however, he was preoccupied in a uniquely imaginative and ingenious way with elaborating the minimalists' preference for basing deterrence on relative risk-taking, resolve, and the balance of interests rather than on the capability to defeat the adversary's fighting capacity. He went further than other minimalists and maximalists before him in applying the psychological factor to warfighting and, through intrawar bargaining, to the conduct and termination of war. This approach was consistent with his abiding conviction, as expressed in *Arms and Influence* (1966), that the effectiveness of violence depends on the skillful exploitation of its potential punitive effect, not on its material destructiveness as such.

When it came to applying a bargaining strategy to strategic nuclear war, Schelling was ambivalent. There was no doubt in his mind that strategic strikes must be restrained and controlled as instruments of diplomatic persuasion rather than directed toward destroying the adversary's fighting capacity or capacity to survive; for, given the growing Soviet capacity to retaliate with its own strategic force, the latter course would be a formula for incurring a senseless catastrophe.

But Schelling was skeptical about concepts of limited strategic warfare that relied on the game-like rationality of bargaining with either measured counterforce increments or setpiece tit-for-tat city exchanges. He saw limited strategic warfare as a competition in risk-taking, conducted through the medium of reprisals, in which the most rationally restrained contestant might lose to the one that seemed somewhat impetuous and unpredictable.[22] Like the RAND maximalists, he applauded Secretary of Defense McNamara's announcement of a strategic damage-limiting strategy (combining reciprocal city-avoidance, counterforce attrition of retaliatory capabilities, and civil defense), but he interpreted this strategy as an exercise in bargaining to end a war through punitive coercion, reserving the ultimate bargaining chips—cities—as hostages, rather than as an exercise in competitive attrition of warfighting capabilities.[23] A limited strategic war, he warned, could not just run down by exhaustion. It had to be brought to an end by the "diplomacy of violence." Provided that U.S. and Soviet strategic forces were sufficiently invulnerable to survive a first strike and inflict unacceptable retaliatory damage on hostage-cities, a strategy of limited punitive retaliation, Schelling believed, would be the best means of bringing a major war with the Soviets to a rational conclusion. Certainly, it was preferable to massive retaliation of any kind.[24]

Schelling shared Albert Wohlstetter's concern about the "delicate balance of terror" that sprang from the vulnerability of U.S. bombers and missiles to a surprise Soviet nuclear attack; but, unlike most maximalists, he emphasized in *The Strategy of Conflict*[25] and in various RAND papers the danger of precipitating such an attack preemptively by making the Soviets fear a surprise attack because of the vulnerability of their retaliatory forces. To obviate the dangers of war inherent in the reciprocal fear of surprise attack, he proposed that mutual deterrence be stabilized through agreed-upon arms limitations and became the intellectual leader of the minimalist school of arms control. He did not subscribe to MAD as a targeting doctrine, but his emphasis on making deterrence and warfighting "non-zero-sum games" implied that U.S. and Soviet interests in stabilizing the nuclear balance and fighting war as though it were a violent form of bargaining were identical—a view that was at the root of MAD and existential deterrence and an anathema to the 100 percent maximalist.

To bridge the logical gap between stabilizing the nuclear balance by making first strikes mutually unprofitable and basing extended deterrence in Europe on a credible U.S. willingness to initiate nuclear war, Schelling propounded the tactic of a nuclear "shot across the bow" and "limited or graduated reprisals"; like Brodie, however, he stopped short of endorsing the idea of a limited nuclear war. Further, he popularized a favorite minimalist notion that the essence of deterrence is not to convince the adversary that aggression is certain to be met by any particular military response designed to make it unprofitable, but to encourage uncertainty about the nature and consequences of response—to "leave something to chance." Far worse from the standpoint of the true maximalists' preoccupation with rationalizing deterrence on the basis of material warfighting capabilities, Schelling argued in *Arms and Influence* (1966) that in a bargaining situation the best deterrent or warfighting tactic might be deliberately to deprive oneself of a choice—that the most rational course might be to convey the appearance of irrationality.

Schelling's ideas and insights about the political and humanitarian advantages of exploiting the psychology of destructive potential while avoiding or restricting the overt use of military capabilities have been appropriated by the minimalists for their own defense policies and strategies. His views on how to stabilize mutual deterrence have been appropriated by arms control enthusiasts of a minimalist disposition. But Schelling's subtle merging of maximalist and minimalist perspectives in his writings tells us more about the problem of rationalizing mitigation of the nuclear dilemma than do the writings of those who fall more clearly on one side or the other of the maximalist/minimalist spectrum.

The Role of the Mitigators

In military strategy the mitigators' ascending influence on public policy as well as on strategic theory took place in the formative years from 1946 to the Vietnam War. The history of their influence is written largely in the works of the new breed of security scholars at the RAND Corporation in Santa Monica and in the policy studies and promotional activities, undertaken by the government or under the leadership of a few prominent men of public affairs, of which Paul Nitze is the outstanding example. In arms control, the mitigators exerted their maximum influence during the 1960s and until the failure to ratify SALT II; the last arms agreement resulted from the strategic arms limitation talks in the 1970s. Their influence emanated largely from defense intellectuals at Harvard and

MIT in Cambridge. The military strategists were mostly maximalists; the arms controllers were mostly minimalists.

The special stimulus to the rise of the strategic mitigators was their opposition to SAC's operational strategy and to Eisenhower's New Look strategy. More broadly, it was their perception of a dangerous gap between the United States' expanding security interests and the domestic political limitations on applying its military potential to support these interests in the face of rapidly growing Soviet nuclear strength, coupled with Soviet superiority in conventional forces in Europe. The mitigators were strategic reformers. Their reform was intended to curb the undiscriminating redundancy in strategic targeting; to moderate the professional military's preoccupation with punitive offensive strategy by fostering more effective defensive denial strategies; to introduce limited nuclear as well as conventional options, including the withholding of civilian and urban-industrial strikes; and to establish a strategy of flexible and controlled responses to limited aggressions in the NATO area and the Third World. Because achievement of these objectives would require an unprecedented expansion of defense expenditures in peacetime, contrary to the ingrained national propensity for retrenching defense expenditures in the absence or aftermath of a crisis or war, the strategic reformers conveyed a sense of great urgency in the face of ominous danger.

The most notable effort of the strategic reformers to rouse the government to meet the challenge of a larger and more flexible defense posture was the official policy study known as NSC 68. Drafted mainly by the Department of State's Policy Planning Staff, this report was spearheaded by Paul Nitze (head of the Policy Planning Staff) and submitted to President Truman, at his request, in April 1950.[26] Although signed by Truman, it was never formally approved as the basis of policy or action because, among other reasons, it would obviously have required a huge defense budget increase when President Truman and his parsimonious secretary of defense, Louis Johnson, were determined to hold this budget to about $13 million. Only with the crash rearmament touched off by the Korean War and, later, with President Kennedy's post-Sputnik program to prevent a missile gap (which did not exist) and to build up limited-war capabilities for Third World contingencies (the only one of which was developing in Vietnam) did it become possible to fund the recommendations of NSC 68.

NSC 68 endorsed the general foreign policy of containment, not only as a defense against Soviet expansion but also as the means of applying counterpressure that would cause the contraction of Soviet control and influence and the moderation of Soviet behavior. The only problem with containment, the report contended, was that the military strength to support it was declining while U.S. security concerns were expanding and Soviet military strength was rapidly mounting. The resulting gap between military strength and international commitments was all the more dangerous because containment really required a sizable margin of military superiority in order to compensate for the natural weaknesses and vulnerabilities of a democracy in maintaining its own security and supporting the security of others during peacetime. By 1954, NSC 68 estimated, the Soviets would have a sufficient nuclear striking capability against the United States to nullify U.S. nuclear superiority and launch a devastating surprise attack. To avoid this perilous situation NSC 68 urged, as a first priority, that the United States strengthen its nuclear capabilities—specifically within the context of a strategy of responding to aggression by using nuclear weapons first, not only by retaliating against a Soviet surprise attack; for a strategy of no-nuclear first-use, if believed, would be an inadequate deterrent unless the United States had overwhelming nuclear superiority. But the broader recommendation of NSC 68, based on the declining utility of any form of nuclear response to aggression, was that the United States "increase as rapidly as possible our general air, ground and sea strength and that of our allies to a point where we are militarily not so heavily dependent on atomic weapons."[27] Above all, the United States must avoid incurring the dilemma of being able to respond to limited, local extensions of Soviet control only with general and nuclear war.

As for relying on the elimination of nuclear weapons under international control of nuclear energy in order to escape the perils of nuclear dependence, NSC 68 virtually dismissed this abolitionist goal as unrealistic and disadvantageous. Only if the free world were so strong politically and economically as to frustrate the Soviet design for world domination could one rely on such disarmament to serve an advantageous peace, even assuming considerable progress in building up the conventional military strength of the free world. Negotiation for disarmament, the report concluded, "is not a possible separate course of action but rather a means of gaining support for a problem of building strength, of recording, where necessary and desirable, progress in the cold war, and of facilitating further progress while helping to minimize the risks of war."[28]

In the 1950s the disarmament solution to the nuclear dilemma more clearly receded into its proper role as propaganda, but under the Eisenhower-Dulles post-Korean retrenchment and reemphasis upon massive retaliation the maximalist position represented in NSC 68 fared no better. Nitze's concern and frustration deepened over the maladies of excessive nuclear dependence. His discontent found an outlet through his participation on the Gaither Committee and his co-authorship of its final report in 1957.[29] As a committee of private experts with a preponderance of RAND personnel, the Gaither Committee was commissioned by President Eisenhower in order to allay the growing controversy over the New Look defense policies incited by the maximalists. It recommended a five-year program with primary emphasis on deterring a surprise attack through less vulnerable and strengthened nuclear offensive capabilities, along with ABMs (to protect SAC bases in the near term and cities in the longer term) and a nationwide fallout-shelter program. But more important than its recommendations, which were ignored, was its explicit underlying premise that massive retaliation was not a credible strategy because it rested on the outmoded assumption of overwhelming U.S. nuclear superiority. Thus, although the report was preoccupied with the enhancement of long-range nuclear capabilities, it recommended augmenting allied forces for limited military operations in order to deter small wars or to suppress them quickly so as to prevent their expansion; it also speculated that if SAC could be made more survivable, this would be "the best time to negotiate from strength, since the U.S. military position vis-à-vis Russia might never be so strong again."[30]

The Gaither Committee's implicit premise about the depreciation of U.S. nuclear preponderance coincided with Nitze's growing skepticism about the utility of basing U.S. national security policy on the capacity to deliver a disarming first strike, as opposed to seeking a stable equilibrium of U.S. and Soviet nuclear capacities to absorb a first strike and retaliate by inflicting unacceptable damage on the enemy.[31] Nevertheless, Nitze was not prepared to write off the value of strategic superiority as a deterrent and as an essential backstop for diplomacy, in some sense, especially in crises.[32] At the same time, he found value in the rising interest during the 1960s in arms control as a complement to a flexible and controlled response strategy intended to stabilize a safer East-West military equilibrium. In the 1970s he became a negotiator of the ABM Treaty and SALT I; then, outside the government, the leading opponent of SALT II; and, in the Reagan administration, the head of arms negotiations concerning the intermediate-range nuclear forces in Europe (INF).

The arms controllers of the 1960s (some of whom could also be considered leading strategists) shared the strategic reformers' objectives; but, impressed by the difficulty, if not impossibility, of retaining the kind of nuclear superiority or attaining the kind of conventional parity that these objectives would demand, they looked to bilateral arms limitation agreements to ease the task of defense programs in achieving the minimal requirements of national security. The arms control movement rose in opposition to the advocates of an unlimited counterforce and warwinning strategy, but also in opposition to the maximalist proponents of ABMs as a nationwide population shield against Soviet attacks. Minimalist arms controllers sought to moderate the arms race, to stabilize the strategic balance on the basis of invulnerable nuclear retaliatory capabilities, and, more broadly, to foster a range of unilateral reciprocal limitations on armed forces and their employment. The arms controllers, like the strategists, were largely successful in selling their ideas to the government, with the encouragement and collaboration of President Kennedy. But although the ABM

Treaty and the SALT I interim agreement were hailed by minimalists as the defeat of maximalism, arms control was not the exclusive property of the minimalists; indeed, the maximalists revealed their political strength when disillusionment with these arms agreements followed the collapse of détente. The abiding influence of the maximalists was foreshadowed in their impact on operational military plans and policies during the 1960s.

The success of the strategic reformers was marked, first, by their influence in getting military planners to qualify their single-minded preoccupation with retaining superiority in a first-strike capability with a comparable concern for acquiring an adequate second-strike (retaliatory) capability. Their most critical immediate objective was to render less vulnerable the air bases and missile bases intended to carry out this capability—a mission in behalf of which Albert Wohlstetter became famous. Second, the strategists' success was marked in the mid-1960s by the transformation of long-range nuclear targeting strategy so as to incorporate limited nuclear options. The third area of success, shared through the efforts of the minimalists as well as the maximalists, was to secure official endorsement by the Kennedy administration of a strategy of flexible and controlled response, designed to decrease dependence on nuclear deterrence in Europe and the Third World.

The roots of these operational successes lay in the intellectual attacks being waged against the orthodoxies of official minimalism. The most prolific and flamboyant publicist of the practical absurdity and immorality of SAC strategy was Herman Kahn. Although his views were generally shared by other maximalists, they were distinguished by the colorful zeal with which he promoted certain special concerns. Particularly notable were his insistence on the value of saving millions of lives out of many more millions of deaths in a strategic nuclear war; his proposal for an emergency capability to counteract Soviet city evacuation with a crash civil and air defense program; his emphasis, in the early 1960s, on the necessity of a credible (later changed to "not incredible") strategic first-strike capability against major Soviet provocations, such as an attack on

Western Europe; and his elaboration of the dynamics of controlled escalation.[33]

During the 1950s, the maximalists' campaign against overreliance on nuclear deterrence (symbolized by "massive retaliation") and for nonnuclear capabilities and strategies of limited war (especially in the Third World) overshadowed their efforts to formulate a strategy of less-than-massive retaliation. But the inspiration for both concerns was the same: the Soviet acquisition of thermonuclear warheads coupled to long-range missiles. In the public eye, Kahn's colorful and controversial indulgence in the details of controlled strategic war overshadowed the more tentative efforts of others to pursue the same strategic goal by enhancing the accuracy and invulnerability of missiles and by improving the command, control, communication, and intelligence-gathering devices (C^3I) for using them with discrimination. The fact that all concepts of limited strategic war attributed central importance to a comprehensive civil defense program—a program always far more unpopular in the nation than massive retaliation ever became—bespoke the lack of public appeal and official attention associated with this strand of mitigation theory. Nevertheless, the strategy of controlled strategic war did gain a momentary and rhetorical official endorsement in Secretary of Defense McNamara's formulation of a damage-limiting strategy in the early 1960s—an endorsement that presaged the elaboration and operational development of the strategy in the 1970s.

The principal lever of influence in changing SAC's all-out warwinning strategy was the single integrated operational target plan (SIOP), created in 1960 as a concession to the concept of flexible and controlled responses. Ostensibly designed to eliminate the redundant duplication of nuclear target plans by competing armed services, the SIOP was in reality the creature of SAC. It planned for an all-out nuclear strike against the USSR, Eastern Europe, and Red China—not only a retaliatory but a preemptive strike, and not only against a Soviet attack on the United States but also against a Soviet attack on Western Europe. With Secretary of Defense McNamara's cooperation, however, the strategic mitigators succeeded in revising the SIOP to support a "controlled response," by permitting both the withholding of strikes against cities and the discrimination among countries targeted, the kinds of counterforce targets, and the explosive yields.

The ultimate triumph of the RAND mitigators was McNamara's articulation of a second-strike counterforce damage-limiting strategy of controlled and flexible nuclear options in a presentation before NATO foreign and defense ministers in Athens in May 1962, and in a commencement address at the University of Michigan in Ann Arbor in June.[34] But this was a limited and ephemeral victory for the maximalists. The damage-limiting strategy did not exclude either urban-industrial targets (which the maximalists wished to be able to avoid for the sake of reciprocal city-avoidance) or strategic nuclear first-strikes (which the maximalists were coming to view as a diminishing asset), and it scarcely altered operational strategic plans. Moreover, even as a criterion for procurement, it soon fell victim to McNamara's scheme to limit SAC's claims on the budget for counterforce capabilities and, simultaneously, to limit ABMs by means of an arms control treaty with the USSR. Nevertheless, both the concept of limited nuclear options and the emphasis on controlled second-strike capabilities survived. In NSDM 242 (1974) and PD 59 (1980), the strategy of controlled and flexible nuclear responses was refined, elaborated, and translated more effectively into the operational plans and measures needed to implement it.

The strategy of mitigation was more successfully and enduringly translated into operational plans, under Secretary McNamara's aegis, in NATO's adoption of MC 14/3 (1967), which incorporated a strategy of initial conventional resistance, followed by nuclear escalation if resistance failed. It also enjoyed much official doctrinal and some operational support as part of President Kennedy's popularization of limited nonnuclear war, including counterinsurgency war, to cope with "wars of national liberation" in the Third World. In the first flush of Kennedy's campaign to revitalize containment, the strategy of flexible and controlled response was propelled into the status of a doctrinal axiom with the fuel of expanded defense expenditures generated by the national reaction to the Soviet orbiting of Sputnik, the alleged missile gap, Khrushchev's Berlin ultimatum, and the perceived threat of wars of national liberation in the Third World.

The influence of the arms controllers on official policy was most marked in the partial nuclear test ban treaty of 1963, the nuclear nonproliferation treaty of 1967, the Antiballistic Missile Treaty (of unrestricted duration), and the SALT I Interim Agreement to freeze strategic nuclear forces. The treaties, in turn, greatly strengthened the hold on civilian and official security specialists of the whole rationale of arms control; in contrast to traditional disarmament, these treaties—as a necessary complement to defense policies—were intended to stabilize mutual deterrence on the basis of an unavoidable situation of mutual national vulnerability to destruction in a nuclear war (subsequently labeled "existential" MAD).

These successes transformed the United States' approach to military strategy and arms control and firmly established the dominance of mitigation over rejection and abolition. But success was accompanied by a growing controversy between the minimalist and maximalist mitigators. This controversy was resolved in favor of the former in the ABM Treaty, but it reemerged with the demise of SALT II and the concomitant collapse of the détente of the early 1970s, only to be absorbed and diffused by the controversies surrounding President Reagan's concept of the strategic defense initiative in the 1980s.

The two schools of mitigation had joined in opposing SAC's targeting doctrine and in advocating a no-cities-option strategy and a capacity to withhold strikes against urban-industrial targets. Both pointed out the difference between the requirements of a first-strike and a second-strike capability, and stressed the importance of an invulnerable second-strike capability for deterring a nuclear attack against the United States. In opposition to the Eisenhower-Dulles strategy of substituting a nuclear response for local resistance, both supported a strategy of flexible and controlled response for NATO and of limited conventional and unconventional warfare in the Third World. But divergences of approach began to appear when the issue of the role of tactical nuclear weapons in extended deterrence arose. These divergences continued to revolve around the issue of NATO's nuclear first-use strategy, although in neither case were the two groups neatly divided.

3

Extended Deterrence

The nuclear dilemma would not be nearly so acute if the United States were not obliged by its vital geopolitical interests to contain Soviet aggression against Europe. If Western Europe were a unified political entity with its own nuclear and conventional forces capable of deterring or defeating a Soviet attack, or even if, as a group of allies with no unified armed forces, it were willing and able to muster an adequate nonnuclear deterrent, the problem of extended deterrence would scarcely exist. But the security of the European allies, from the beginning, has been critically dependent on U.S. protection, which, in turn, has depended on a U.S. pledge to initiate the use of nuclear weapons against an attack that could not be withstood conventionally. Consequently, the extension of the United States' nuclear deterrence to the protection of Europe has raised the twin chronic problems: The United States must reassure the allies that it will use nuclear weapons in their behalf but also that it will not precipitate their destruction if deterrence fails.

In the face of Soviet conventional superiority and the steady growth of Soviet nuclear-strike capabilities against the United States as well as the allies, the United States has resorted to a long succession of measures to enhance the credibility and acceptability of extended deterrence; but the underlying sources of these problems remain. Therefore, no aspect of the nuclear dilemma has been more fruitful of plans and programs, of issues and controversies, in military strategy and arms control policy, than extended deterrence. No aspect has so continually engaged the efforts of mitigators, both maximalist and minimalist.

Logically, the fundamental solution to NATO's dilemma was to replace U.S. extended deterrence with a European-managed deterrent. Apparently, Eisenhower saw merit in this idea.[35] Herman Kahn proposed a European Strategic Defense Community to implement a doctrine of "proportionate nuclear reprisal."[36] However, all official proposals for a European nuclear role, such as SACEUR, Norstad's "NATO nuclear force," or the ill-famed Multilateral Nuclear Force (MLF), fell far short of European management of nuclear deterrence.[37] In fact, such measures of nuclear sharing were intended as a substitute for European nuclear control and as a barrier to the proliferation of independent national nuclear forces beyond those of France and Great Britain.

In political reality, it is hard to imagine the existence of a collective European nuclear force without a united Europe to give it central military and political control. But despite some early visions that the process of economic coalescence might spill over into security relations, true unification eluded even the economic process. Lesser measures of nuclear sharing ran afoul of the politics of the French and British nuclear forces and the insuperable problem of German participation or exclusion. Consequently, mitigation of the dilemma of extended nuclear deterrence has depended on strengthening NATO's conventional resistance capabilities, on excluding the first-use of nuclear weapons, and on developing a strategy of limited nuclear warfare. The first course has received much assent, although only inadequate implementation. Proposals for no-nuclear first-use persist, in conjunction with strengthening conventional defense; but they contravene the politics of allied cohesion and are stymied by the economic and political obstacles to raising the nuclear threshold. The development of a convincing strategy for the limited use of nuclear weapons has evaded all private and official efforts to achieve it.

The earliest effort to mitigate the nuclear dilemma at the core of extended deterrence came in the aftermath of the Korean War with the pledge to keep six U.S. divisions on Western Europe's central front and to create an allied military organization (NATO) commanded by an American general. This effort was soon followed by the expedient of compensating the shortfall in meeting NATO's conventional force goals with the new battlefield (or tactical) nuclear weapons. In 1952 official plans were approved to supplement SAC's cumbersome atomic bombs, deliverable mostly by large bombers from vulnerable overseas bases, with short-range German-based tactical nuclear weapons using new technology for smaller warheads delivered by rockets, artillery, and aircraft. The strategic impetus behind the nuclearization of NATO forces came from the momentary fear of a Soviet or Soviet-proxy attack following the Korean invasion and the subsequent failure of the allies to meet the ambitious Lisbon conventional force goals, which in turn were intended to meet the specified military requirements for a forward defense of NATO's central front. Well suited to the New Look's effort to get "more bang for the buck," tactical nuclear weapons were destined to become a center of controversy when the Eisenhower-Dulles strategy came under attack by the mitigators. But although NATO absorbed an expanding arsenal of tactical nuclear weapons in subsequent years, the controversy over how to use them and how much to rely on them has never been resolved, even among the mitigators.

From the maximalist standpoint, prominent RAND civilian strategists, such as William Kaufmann and Alain Enthoven, became increasingly skeptical during the 1960s of the military utility of tactical nuclear weapons and of the feasibility of limiting their use to any significant extent. They argued for drawing the line (the "firebreak") between conventional and nuclear weapons as clearly as possible and stressed the necessity of strengthening conventional denial capabilities.[38] Among those who regarded a nuclear response to Soviet aggression as the only alternative to conventional defeat or massive retaliation, some favored limited strategic rather than tactical nuclear strikes as a means of deterrence and rational warfighting on the grounds that strategic weapons were less vulnerable and easier to keep under political control.[39] But this was before Soviet strategic retaliatory capabilities virtually ended U.S. strategic superiority in any useful sense.

It was on the role of tactical nuclear weapons that Bernard Brodie first split with the maximalists, among whom he had been one of the earliest to oppose indiscriminate strategic targeting. Brodie believed that an emphasis on a conventional-nuclear firebreak and stronger conventional forces (1) under-estimated, and might diminish, the deterrent power of tactical nuclear weapons and (2) overestimated the Western capacity to offset Soviet conventional superiority by nuclear deterrence. But like Kahn, Schelling, and other mitigators, he argued for the necessity and feasibility of nuclear escalatory steps, not as part of a limited nuclear warwinning strategy (such as Henry Kissinger advocated for a few years in the late 1950s and early 1960s)[40] but as measures of intrawar deterrence to bring the war to a rational end.

Brodie's position turned out to correspond with the political realities of NATO, which led to allied agreement to MC 14/3 in 1967—constructed to be a deliberately ambiguous com-promise between U.S. pressure to raise the nuclear threshold and European determination not to raise it too far. In MC 14/3 the decision was made that the first-use of nuclear weapons, in case conventional resistance failed, would be an escalatory strike with tactical nuclear weapons, not a full-scale tactical nuclear war. Strategic nuclear exchanges were reserved for the final stage if escalation failed to produce a satisfactory negotiated settlement. Nevertheless, the role of tactical nuclear weapons in extended deterrence remained one of the most persistent and insoluble issues in U.S. strategic thought. One mark of its intractability is that the minimalists and the max-imalists were both adversaries and allies in their views on NATO's strategy of nuclear first-use.

Minimalists and maximalists have all strongly agreed that raising the nuclear threshold by increasing NATO's capability for conventional resistance at the forward line in central Europe is an indispensable measure of mitigation; but most mitigators in either group have taken the view that, for the sake of deterrence as well as allied cohesion, the option of nuclear escalation must be preserved in the absence of any politically acceptable and militarily feasible way of supplanting it with conventional denial capabilities. The propensity of the minimalists has been to accept the strategic contradictions that results and make the most of them, as this approach would at least avoid futile and politically unsettling efforts to overcome them by competing with Soviet warfighting capabilities. The propensity of the maximalists has been to downgrade the popular estimate of Warsaw Pact conventional superiority, insist on the material and economic possibility of raising the nuclear threshold at least to the point of thirty-days' conventional resistance, and call for advanced conventional technology (principally, precision-guided munitions coupled with C^3I) to offset Soviet military advantages.

Since the late 1960s, however, substantial increases in Soviet conventional capabilities (linked with a change of military doctrine to allow for an initial conventional option and even a large-scale conventional war), as well as large increases in absolute and relative Soviet nuclear capabilities from short-range to medium-range weapons in the European theater, have further shaken the mitigators' confidence in NATO's capacity to alleviate the dilemmas of extended deterrence through the familiar ambiguities of nuclear first-use in the flexible-response strategy. This loss of faith in flexible response was dramatized by Henry Kissinger's famous renunciation at Brussels in September 1979 of further declarations of U.S. willingness to incur the penalties of nuclear war in order to protect the allies.[41] Although Kissinger's remedy at the time was to increase strategic counterforce and conventional resistance capabilities, not to abandon nuclear-first-use, some minimalists and maximalists reached the latter prescription on the basis of the same premises.

THE QUESTION OF FIRST-USE

Fred Iklé, several years out of office as director of ACDA (1973–1977), stated most starkly the maximalist case for a military posture of no-nuclear first-use, although he held that given such a posture, a declaration of no-nuclear first-use would be futile or worse.[42] His principal point was that vastly increased Soviet nuclear capabilities made first-use militarily and psychologically disadvantageous. He believed that NATO's nuclear-first-use might well be an adequate deterrent against a Soviet military assault, but he was afraid that it would be revealed as an empty bluff in an acute crisis. If the Alliance actually had to face the prospect of using the deterrent, the Soviets would exploit the Western fear that nuclear war is mutual suicide in order to extract some political concession in a contest of national will. To avoid this danger the Western countries would have to regard nuclear weapons, not as psychological instruments to avoid war, but as military instruments to fight an adversary if deterrence failed. Given the loss of U.S. nuclear superiority, this would mean that nuclear weapons should serve to improve a second-strike capability; similarly, conventional forces should be strengthened and the United States and its allies should prepare to respond to a Soviet conventional attack with an all-out military buildup.

Writing in the 1980s, Herman Kahn reminded his readers that he had been in favor of a no-nuclear first-use policy for twenty years. Like the targeting of enemy cities to avoid the problems of discriminating counterforce planning, he regarded the first-use of nuclear weapons to defend Western Europe, "simply to avoid the more complicated capabilities, plans, and costs required for improved conventional defenses," as immoral.[43] At the same time, he reasoned that to retain the credibility of extended deterrence under a no-first-use policy would require both a credible ability to counter a conventional attack conventionally and a not-incredible counterforce first-strike capability, in addition to a rational and morally justifiable nuclear second-strike capability. He believed that none of these requirements were adequately addressed by the abolitionists, who were currently advocating the renunciation of nuclear first-use.[44]

It was not the maximalists (such as Iklé, Kaufmann, and Kahn) but the minimalists who made opposition to nuclear first-use prominent in the marketplace of strategic ideas. In 1982 McGeorge Bundy, George Kennan, Robert McNamara, and Gerard Smith (who quickly, in deprecating memory of China's Cultural Revolution, became known as the Gang of Four) made the much more widely noted minimalist case for both a declaration and a posture of no-nuclear first-use for NATO.[45] They shared the standard mitigationist position that this policy would require strengthened conventional forces. They, too, started from the premise that the United States' loss of nuclear superiority made nuclear first-use a strategy of mutual suicide. But they were less worried than the maximalists either that this strategy was a bluff or that it was ineffective as a deterrent. Indeed, their confidence in existential nuclear deterrence convinced them that so long as these weapons existed, no declaration of nuclear nonuse could guarantee the Soviets or the Western powers that the outbreak of large-scale conventional war would not lead to the use of nuclear weapons. Their principal motivation for such a declaration was the fear that nuclear weapons might actually be used and that they would "threaten the peace of the world"; their concern, stimulated by the INF deployment crisis, was that the nuclear first-use policy was jeopardizing the "political coherence" and "internal health" of the Alliance. In addition, they hoped that a posture and policy of no-first-use would prod the allies into creating effective conventional forces, obviate the pressure for escalation dominance, reduce the requirements for matching Soviet modernization of major nuclear systems, open the way toward the reduction of nuclear armaments on both sides, and allay European anxieties that underlay pressure for nuclear armaments and nuclear-free zones.

Equally revealing of the difficulty of reconciling the conflicting strategic objectives embodied in NATO's nuclear first-use policy was the stance of those mitigators who confessed that the policy was illogical but nonetheless asserted the necessity of keeping it. Similarly, Richard Betts presented a devastating analysis of all the things that are wrong with the policy, argued that abandoning or renouncing the policy would only make things worse, and concluded that nuclear first-use is strategically and politically right, even though it is a "White Lie" or a "Grand Illusion."[46] A certain amount of incoherence, he argued, is the price of allied solidarity, which is itself a more powerful deterrent than any conceivable military improvements could be.

The ABM Debate

Even more important as a source of divergence between maximalists and minimalists was the ABM issue.[47] ABMs—ground-based interceptor missiles (with nuclear warheads in the period before the ABM Treaty of 1972)—were the first operational weapons to grow out of the initial U.S. strategic defense program. This program began in the late 1940s as a counter to the anticipated threat of Soviet long-range bombers. It was given a new emphasis and a broader technological scope (including even anti-boost-phase devices) in Project Defender (1958), which was intended to counter the threat of Soviet intercontinental ballistic missiles (ICBMs). From the beginning, ABMs were controversial within the official defense community and among scientists and engineers; but they did not become the object of a major public debate until late 1963 and 1964, when nuclear scientists, such as Jerome Wiesner, President Kennedy's scientific adviser, began opposing the development and deployment of ABMs on the grounds that they would precipitate an arms race that would upset the strategic equilibrium and ruin the prospects of arms control.

To the maximalists, the appeal of ABMs, in the 1950s and 1960s, was the prospect they offered of the United States' recovering and retaining something of the invulnerability from Soviet nuclear attack and, concomitantly, the nuclear superiority that the country had enjoyed when it had a monopoly of strategic nuclear weapons deliverable on the adversary's homeland. Their hope was not that ABMs would enable the United States to return to isolation in Fortress America, as European opponents of ABMs feared—they shared the postwar American view that the security of Western Europe was integral to U.S. security—but that strategic defense would strengthen nuclear deterrence by protecting the nation from Soviet bombers and missiles and save lives if deterrence failed. Although not isolationist, the maximalists' interest in ABMs was nevertheless strongly U.S. centered. This was indicated by the fact that, with very few exceptions, the maximalists based their case for defending the United States not on the plausible argument that an ABM program would strengthen the credibility of extended nuclear deterrence in Europe but, rather, on the objective of limiting damage to Americans. Insofar as European concerns figured in the ABM debate of the 1960s, they pertained to the possibility, noted by ABM supporters, that the degradation of U.S. nuclear strikes by Soviet ABMs would weaken extended deterrence and therefore stimulate European (i.e., German) nuclear proliferation.[48]

The most avid promoters of ABMs, such as Army General Earle Wheeler and Edward Teller, stressed the importance of an ABM program in order to retain technological superiority in warfighting capabilities over the Soviets—a superiority they considered an indispensable compensation for Soviet stealth and aggressiveness. Their argument for technological prowess was reinforced by the first Soviet deployment of the Galosh ABMs around Moscow in 1964. In that year Donald Brennan, after discovering the extent of Soviet ABM deployments, reappraised the effectiveness of the technology and abandoned his arms control orientation, based on stabilizing retaliatory offensive capabilities and opposing defensive deployments, in favor of a "thick" (i.e., nationwide) ABM deployment. Thereafter, until his suicide in 1980, he became one of the most ardent champions of the concept of restructuring deterrence to depend on a strong proportion of strategic defensive to offensive capabilities. Like that of Teller, however, Brennan's advocacy of ABMs was based essentially on the damage-limiting, lifesaving concept that Herman Kahn persistently promoted against the weight of scientific and strategic opinion: the concept that it is worth saving millions of lives in a nuclear exchange, even if many more millions will be lost. And he coupled this concept with the view that it is safer and more effective, as well as more humane, to base deterrence on a response to aggression that ensures one's own nation's survival than on a response that ensures destruction of the enemy.[49]

Ironically, the objective that made ABMs so attractive to the maximalists was precisely the objective that spelled defeat for the pro-ABM campaign in the 1960s: the protection of people, not missiles and bombers. In retrospect, one wonders why this objective was so dominant, especially since the early

ABM technology—even after the 1962 Pacific tests indicated the potential of an urban defense system—was better adapted to enhancing deterrence by providing a partial defense of military bases and facilities than to protecting people by area defense. The answer lies partly in the fact that the compelling image of surprise attack, which ABMs were supposed to counter, was derived from the memory of city-busting in World War II. Correspondingly, Americans tended to measure the strategic threat to national security largely in terms of the nation's shocking loss of invulnerability to Soviet city-busting. Moreover, in the 1960s many maximalists still believed that a credible strategic first-strike capability was an essential and feasible deterrent; and this deterrent clearly depended on limiting Soviet retaliatory damage. But equally important was the simple fact that, aside from a few experts, neither the maximalists nor the minimalists were yet much worried about the vulnerability of U.S. bombers and missiles to a Soviet strike, given the weakness of Soviet strike forces and the redundant strength of U.S. retaliatory forces. Most experts assured the public that there were cheaper and easier ways to protect these forces (such as concealing them in submarines and hardening their bases) than trying to knock out missiles with missiles.

Nevertheless, the rationale of protecting people flew in the face of an emerging consensus among minimalists that, as Soviet strategic capabilities increased, the hope for stable mutual deterrence and a moderated arms race would reside in the reciprocal recognition by the superpowers that the only realistic objective of their nuclear forces was the protection of retaliatory capabilities while national populations were unavoidably vulnerable to mutual assured destruction. This strategic concept was supported by the prevailing technical assessment that the available technology—the Nike-X (consisting of the short-range Sprint, the longer-range area-defense Spartan interceptor, and a new family of radars), which was launched as the Sentinel system in 1967, could not prevent the offensive capabilities (especially given the new penetration aids and MIRVed warheads) from destroying cities more easily and cheaply than ABMs could protect them. Moreover, the lifesaving rationale (the view that it is important to save as many lives as possible in a nuclear holocaust) conflicted with the American disinclination to think about the unthinkable—the American distaste for calculating quantitative distinctions about such absolute horrors as nuclear war. Thus, the fact that advocacy of ABM deployments was generally linked to passive civil defense further condemned the concept of active strategic defense, in the American outlook, as being slightly crazy and possibly provocative.

Nor were the other, less emotion-laden arguments for ABMs any more persuasive:

1. The Sentinel system would provide a thin defense against a Chinese attack or an accidental nuclear attack. There was little public concern about either of these contingencies, which seemed to have been invented as afterthoughts in any case.
2. ABMs would deny the Soviet Union the psychological and political advantage that would accrue from a monopoly of strategic defense. This argument lost what persuasiveness it had when hopes arose that the Soviets might accept a freeze on ABMs.
3. ABMs would stabilize mutual deterrence by inhibiting either side, but especially the USSR, from thinking that the other could not survive a surprise attack. This view could not compete with the belief that the best protection against a surprise attack was an arms agreement to ensure the invulnerability of retaliatory forces that would make such an attack irrational.
4. ABMs would facilitate arms control by alleviating American fears of technological breakthroughs in offensive weapons and by providing insurance against Soviet violations of an arms agreement, which might upset the military equilibrium. Proponents of arms control, however, were committed to cooperative constraints on offensive weapons and were therefore opposed to the competitive deployment of defensive weapons.

The central weakness of all the pro-ABM arguments was that they seemed to promise little or nothing in terms of strengthening deterrence as opposed to limiting damage if deterrence should fail. In contrast, minimalist opponents of ABMs had a popular position that promised both strong deterrence and moderation of the arms race. They defended mutual assured destruction as the essence of deterrence and the key to stability of the military balance. In the atmosphere of pre-détente that suffused the late 1960s, it was easy to believe that the strategic status quo was the basis of security and that any new weapons system that changed the status quo was dangerous. It was hard to believe that the protection of people could improve deterrence. Anyway, the scientists said that it would always be much easier for the offense to strike cities than for the defense to shield them. The effort to protect the nation, it was argued, would only escalate the arms race without enhancing national security. If ABMs made the Soviets feel more secure, this was no threat to the United States. That sense of security would only increase their satisfaction with the status quo. But if one were worried about Soviet ABMs, the solution would be to ban them in an arms agreement, not to precipitate an arms race by destroying U.S. ABMs.

In these arguments, minimalism merged with finite deterrence in seeming to endorse the morally dubious principle that the best assurance against war lies in the least protection of people from war's devastation. In the 1960s, however, the opponents of strategic defense felt no need to defend their position on moral grounds. In the end, it was neither moral nor strategic considerations but the simple cost-effectiveness argument—the argument that strategic defense could not compete with strategic offense when it came to protecting rather than killing people—that proved decisive in defeating proponents of a national shield against a Soviet attack. Certainly this was the main thrust of Secretary of Defense McNamara's successful effort to limit the ABM program to a thin defense against a Chinese attack. However, the ABM debate did not turn on cost-effectiveness alone; it reflected and accentuated a fundamental difference of orientation toward coping with the nuclear dilemma.

Anti-ABM scientists (Jerome Wiesner, Hans Bethe, Isidor Rabi, Herbert York, Richard Garwin, Wolfgang Panofsky,

Jeremy Stone, Herbert ["Pete"] Scoville, and others) lent their expertise to the view that ABMs would not "work"—in other words, that they would not actually protect cities because it would always be easier for missiles to get through than for ballistic missile defenses to keep them out. But it was the philosophical and emotional core of their argument—the view that nuclear weapons were unsuited to any purpose except deterrence—that attracted a broad spectrum of those most anxious about the dangers of the nuclear arms race and most opposed to nuclear weapons as instruments of warfare. By putting the nuclear dilemma into the forefront of controversy, the ABM debate completed the transformation of some of the staunchest antinuclear critics into advocates of a strategy of deterrence based upon equating MAD with the disutility of nuclear weapons, as opposed to a counterforce damage-limiting strategy intended to make nuclear deterrence rational to carry out. Aligned with these critics in opposition to the ABM were many minimalists who did not share the aversion of finite-deterrence advocates to counterforce or to the protection of people in principle. McNamara, for example, was a strong supporter of counterforce superiority and civil defense. But the finer distinctions of strategic reasoning tended to get lost in the heat of the debate.

By the same token, the ABM debate impelled maximalists, such as Albert Wohlstetter, to stress their philosophical and emotional opposition to the concept of mutual assured destruction, which they condemned (with the acronym MAD) as perversely irrational and inhumane. Their antipathy to MAD was further incited by the coupling of the argument for leaving people vulnerable to retaliatory destruction with the criticism of a counterforce warfighting strategy as a stimulant to the "action-reaction" process, which was said to underlie the "mad momentum" of the arms race. Maximalists condemned these phrases, popularized by Secretary McNamara, as proof of the minimalists' lack of realism—perhaps with special bitterness because McNamara's brief endorsement of a counterforce damage-limiting strategy in 1962 had so quickly been abandoned when he lost faith in the feasibility of limiting nuclear exchanges and became concerned with the inflationary effect of a counterforce strategy on defense expenditures. In reality, as subsequent insiders' accounts revealed, McNamara's endorsement of MAD was intended as a standard of sufficiency to limit procurement, not as a doctrine for employing strategic forces, in which the United States still enjoyed superior numbers aimed at an abundance of counterforce targets. Contrary to the maximalists' sweeping condemnation of MAD, most minimalists were as appalled by the concept of finite countercity (or exclusively "countervalue") deterrence as were the maximalists. But the ABM debate pertained to more than just a weapons program and defense expenditures. At stake were competing paradigms and the contrasting value judgments associated with them.

The victory of the minimalists' paradigm was finally assured by the linkage of arms control to MAD. McNamara secured this linkage when, in his notable San Francisco address of September 1967, he coupled the standard MAD arguments against a full-scale ABM deployment (although he endorsed a limited deployment for a thin defense against a Chinese nuclear attack) with an appeal for an East-West strategic arms limitation agreement contingent upon the limitation of ABMs. This effort to limit ABMs in the context of a bilateral agreement with Moscow initially failed when Alexi Kosygin resisted President Johnson's effort to sell it at the Glassboro, New Jersey, summit meeting in 1967, arguing that ABMs could not be destabilizing because they were purely defensive weapons designed to protect people. However, the Soviets subsequently changed their minds and accepted the deal during the Nixon administration. They did so not out of any belief in the benefits of mutual vulnerability (a notion quite contrary to the Soviet military outlook), but partly to stop the newly designated Safeguard ABM program, in which they feared the United States had a technological advantage, and partly because they calculated that the new Soviet ICBMs with multiple independently targetable reentry vehicles (MIRVs) would be a more cost-effective way of implementing their damage-limiting strategy.

Ironically, the victory of the minimalists in the ABM Treaty was assured by the Nixon administration's support of an ABM deployment program based on the rationale of protecting missiles (against the new Soviet SS-9 ICBMs) rather than people. This rationale was not only more salable; it also provided the United States with a bargaining chip that helped persuade Moscow to restrict rather than compete in ABM deployments. Although President Nixon and his advisers were even less enthusiastic proponents of MAD than McNamara, the ABM Treaty codified, sanctified, and bilateralized the concept of stabilizing deterrence on the basis of mutual vulnerability to retaliatory destruction. It marked the triumph of the minimalist approach of the Cambridge school of arms control, which held that the best guarantee of peace lay in invulnerable second-strike retaliatory capabilities against vulnerable national populations. And it signaled the obsolescence of Herman Kahn's goal of a credible or not-incredible first-strike capability to deter and fight major Soviet provocations short of a direct attack on the United States.

The defeat of a full-scale ABM deployment program, however, was only a conditional and temporary defeat for the maximalist approach to the nuclear dilemma. The abiding influence of this approach was soon manifested in official adoption of the concept of limited strategic nuclear options.

LIMITED STRATEGIC NUCLEAR OPTIONS

Despite the creation of the SIOP and the unremitting efforts of RAND mitigators to limit and diversify strategic war plans and bring them under rational political control, operational plans continued into the 1970s to reflect SAC's preference for a massive retaliatory strike—whether in response to conventional aggression in Europe or to a Soviet nuclear attack on the United States—against a list of over 20,000 possible targets, a number seemingly limited only by the growing U.S. target-killing capability. McNamara's temporary acceptance of a damage-limiting strategy with a no-cities option marked the triumph of William Kaufmann's efforts to rationalize strategic nuclear planning; but the secretary's skepticism about the feasibility of significantly limiting nuclear exchanges, his budgetary concern about the proliferation of counterforce capabilities,

NATO's negative response to McNamara's new doctrine, and the emerging popularity of the concept of MAD led to the abandonment of efforts to incorporate an operationally significant strategy of limited nuclear options soon after its apparent adoption.

It was President Nixon's accession to office and the mounting concern about the growth of Soviet MIRVed ICBM striking power (which Paul Nitze and others interpreted as a drive for nuclear superiority) that gave counterforce damage-limitation and limited strategic nuclear options a new life in the 1970s— these factors and the growing accuracy of missiles, coupled with improved C^3I. It was President Nixon, in collaboration with his new national security advisor, Henry Kissinger, who redefined the rationale for strategic nuclear strategy and sufficiency to require MAD *plus* a considerable counterforce capability—a rationale that all subsequent administrations have followed. The *plus* was implicit in the rhetorical question posed in his 1970 Report to Congress: "Should a President in the event of a nuclear attack be left with the single option of ordering the mass destruction of enemy civilians, in the face of the certainty that it would be followed by the mass slaughter of Americans?"[50]

Nixon's endorsement of a flexible counterforce strategy to supplement a capability to deliver assured retaliatory destruction was a welcome signal to the maximalists that MAD, as an operational targeting doctrine, had been condemned to death. Accordingly, RAND maximalists flocked to the execution. Pointing to the relentless Soviet pursuit of a nuclear warwinning capability while U.S. strategic and arms control policies remained enthralled by the fancy that mutual assured destruction was the basis for moderating the arms race and stabilizing deterrence, they reached a new peak of condemnation of MAD on moral as well as expediential grounds. This time there were few real finite-deterrence advocates left— found only among the beleaguered defenders of SALT and the desperate opponents of large counterforce programs to close the "window of vulnerability" (i.e., the vulnerability of U.S. ICBMs to a first strike by Soviet ICBMs). But there were also far fewer advocates of an all-out counterforce warwinning capability.

Given these trends in strategic thought and the development of more accurate missiles with a greater capacity to limit collateral damage, the time was ripe for implementing a strategy of controlled strategic war. Given the maximalists' campaign against the targeting of cities, the proponents of controlled strategic war were now bound to confine limited nuclear strikes to counterforce targets. However, the natural concomitant of such a strategy—civil defense—was not even mentioned. Never popular, it had apparently died (without the possibility of resurrection) in the overwhelming popular opposition to President Kennedy's civil defense program, which unfortunately was keyed to backyard shelters.

When former RAND economist James Schlesinger was appointed by Nixon as director of the CIA and then as secretary of defense, the maximalists once again had in office a proponent of a limited no-cities counterforce strategy. Borrowing from the work of a two-year study in the Pentagon, headed by "Johnny" Foster, Schlesinger announced in 1974 the so-called Schlesinger doctrine (officially designated NSDM-242), which was actually initiated by the previous secretary of defense, Melvin Laird. This document instituted a revised SIOP with a wide spectrum of targets of different categories, intended to facilitate selective strikes (including the avoidance of residential concentrations) to suit different sets of military and political circumstances. Although publicly justified more on humanitarian than on strategic grounds, the Schlesinger doctrine was conceived as the basis of more effective and politically rational warfighting in order to strengthen deterrence as well as to fight aggression if deterrence failed.

In 1980 President Carter's secretary of defense, Harold Brown, incorporated this approach to flexible and controlled nuclear responses in Presidential Directive 59 (PD-59), which elaborated NSDM-242 in the context of a "countervailing strategy" designed to deny the Soviets victory (in their eyes) by appropriate means at every level of attack feasible.[51] Some proponents of limited nuclear options, including Schlesinger, thought that PD-59 carried the concept of warfighting too far in calling for measures to meet such unlikely contingencies as a protracted nuclear war and in prescribing such provocative options as targeting the Soviet military and political leadership (a proposed method that soon entered the strategic lexicon under the gruesome name of "decapitation"). Minimalist opponents of a full-scale damage-limiting strategy charged that PD-59 was tantamount to a dangerous and unrealistic nuclear warwinning strategy.[52] Europeans voiced the familiar anxiety that the presidential directive envisioned fighting a nuclear war that might be limited from the superpowers' standpoint but not from theirs.

Actually, Secretary Brown hedged this refined version of the strategy of flexible and controlled nuclear responses with a number of qualifications. He dissociated it from the idea of winning a nuclear war, striking first, or nullifying Soviet retaliatory capabilities. He expressed serious doubts that either side could gain an advantage in a protracted nuclear war or even engage in limited nuclear exchanges that would stop short of reaching the level of maximum destruction. Decapitation, he explained, was an option that the United States should have only in the event that escalation control failed.[53] The objective of the countervailing strategy, he insisted, was to implement deterrence—especially the deterrence of limited Soviet nuclear attacks—with more flexible, not more devastating, responses; and to halt any nuclear exchange before it reached catastrophic proportions. Reiterating a central minimalist concept, he declared in his Annual Report for Fiscal Year (FY) 1981 that "in adopting and implementing this policy we have no more illusions than our predecessors that a nuclear war could be closely and surgically controlled. There are, of course, great uncertainties about what would happen if nuclear weapons were ever again used. These uncertainties, combined with the catastrophic results sure to follow from a maximum escalation of the exchange, are an essential element of deterrence."[54]

These qualifications, far from convincing minimalist opponents of PD-59 of the utility of limited nuclear options, only confirmed their view of the irrationality of efforts to base the efficacy of nuclear deterrence on the utility of waging nuclear war. Secretary Brown's carefully crafted nuances did, however, capture the essence of one maximalist consensus that remains an integral component of nuclear strategy: the consensus that the primary objective of limiting nuclear options must be not only to dissuade Soviet leaders from undertaking limited as well as all-out nuclear attacks and to prevent them from intimidating the Western allies with their capability for such attacks, but also, if deterrence should fail, to save millions of lives while terminating war at as low a level and on terms as favorable as possible.

4

The Decline of Arms Control

RENEWAL OF THE ABM DEBATE

The incorporation of PD-59 into the SIOP indicated the strength of maximalist influence, notwithstanding the minimalist victory achieved in the ABM Treaty. This strength was based, in part, on the capacity of more accurate missiles to lend credence to a counterforce damage-limiting strategy intended to moderate the unconscionable potential devastation of nuclear retaliation. But in the general euphoria generated by the ABM Treaty, arms control, based on the inescapable vulnerability of national populations to second-strike destruction, was a far more widely appealing method of mitigating the nuclear dilemma than moderating the costs of the failure of deterrence.

Among the experts, however, faith in arms control as a guarantee of a safe and stable military equilibrium was badly shaken by the continued growth of Soviet nuclear strength and the growing vulnerability of U.S. ICBMs. This development refuted the explicit premise of the ABM Treaty that preserving the status quo in strategic defense capabilities would not upset the balance in strategic offensive capabilities. The resulting blow to the prevailing faith in arms control did far more to stimulate the recrudescence of maximalism than the technical advances in missilery. Indeed, it underlay a revival of the ABM debate at the end of the 1970s.

To understand the new debate we must reconsider the end of the old one, because that debate significantly changed the terms of the case for strategic defense. By the time the ABM debate reached its peak in the summer and fall of 1969, the strategic rationale for ABMs had changed. It changed when the incoming Nixon administration announced that the principal rationale of the ABM program, now called Safeguard, would be the protection of missiles. This change was due partly to the failure of the area-defense argument and partly to the adverse public reaction to the decision to deploy ABMs near some cities; but it was largely a result of the fact that a growing number of Soviet ICBMs (SS-9s) in the latter half of the 1960s began to threaten the survivability of U.S. ICBMs. The principal argument for ABMs, therefore, came to be an enhanced version of the familiar and popular deterrence strategy of nuclear retaliation. This and the bargaining chip argument—Nixon's argument that the Safeguard program was necessary to induce Soviet acceptance of an ABM limitation—largely resolved the policy differences between minimalists and maximalists. These changes in the pro-ABM position led to the East-West trade-off embodied in the ABM Treaty and the Interim Agreement of SALT I, the latter of which was superseded by agreement on the unratified SALT II. Both the treaty and the agreement essentially put a ceiling on existing strategic nuclear programs.

Consequently, when maximalist advocates of ABMs renewed their active advocacy, they did so on the grounds that ABMs were necessary to protect missiles, not that they were necessary to protect people. The fact that the Soviets, by putting MIRVs on new ICBMs (within limits set by SALT I and II), greatly increased the vulnerability of U.S. ICBMs provided the proponents of ABMs with a persuasive confirmation of the anti-missiles argument. This turn of events, together with the fatal impact on détente of Soviet opportunism in the Third World, brought the arms control process to a halt. During his final months in office, President Carter felt compelled to withdraw SALT II from the ratification process, although both he and his successor, President Reagan, decided to adhere to the provisions as long as the Soviets reciprocated.

The abortion of the strategic arms limitation process was partly the result of disillusionment with the popular expectation, encouraged by President Nixon and Henry Kissinger, that strategic arms negotiation and agreement would be the centerpiece of greatly improved East-West relations in an "era of negotiations." The general idea, although not consistently applied, was that Soviet interest in an arms agreement codifying military parity with the United states could be linked to Soviet observance of rules of mutual restraint, as formulated in the 1972 Moscow agreement on Basic Principles of Mutual Relations. This expectation died in the Third World, at the hands of a succession of opportunistic Soviet projections of military power and political influence from Angola to Vietnam, South Yemen, and Ethiopia, culminating in the invasion of Afghanistan. This "arc of crisis," as President Carter's national security advisor, Zbigniew Brzezinski, called it, simply fulfilled a principal Soviet objective of détente, which Soviet leaders had openly avowed: to facilitate the advancement of socialism against the outposts of imperialism in an atmosphere of peaceful coexistence. But, of course, the American authors and constituents of détente had never regarded détente, and would never have embraced it, as a backstop for Soviet expansion in the Third World.

THE "WINDOW OF VULNERABILITY"

Simultaneously, and more directly contributing to the shattering of arms control expectations, was the rechanneling of the arms race, which undermined the military balance that SALT was supposed to codify. The United States had signed the ABM Treaty with the expectation (which was embodied in its preamble, its negotiating history, and a stated American understanding) that substantial reductions of strategic nuclear weapons would follow. Instead, because SALT I limited launchers, not warheads, and because it left MIRVs unrestricted (and because SALT II only partially corrected this loophole), the Soviets were legally able to multiply the striking power of their heavy throwweight SS-18s and SS-19s. Hypothetically, then, they could destroy 90 percent or more of U.S. land-based missiles on a first strike while reserving enough of their own strategic capability to inflict assured destruction. Against this capability to kill U.S. hardened ICBMs, the only politically and economically acceptable response the U.S. government could come up with, after failing to sell to Congress several other basing modes (notably, the "race track" and "dense-pack"), was funding the development of the MIRVed MX missile in silos and, for deployment at the end of the century, the mobile single-warhead Midgetman on airbases. But budgetary constraints and technological uncertainties seemed bound to keep deployment of these missiles far short of a level that would restore the invulnerability of the land-based leg of the strategic triad.

The maximalist reaction to this predicament, championed most volubly by the Committee on the Present Danger, with Paul Nitze in the lead, was to point with alarm at the open "window of vulnerability" and place the blame on the SALT agreements—not only for failing to limit the lifting power (or "throwweight") of heavy missiles (because this gave the Soviets a numerical advantage in MIRVs) but also for encouraging a decade of declining defense expenditures while the Soviets raced ahead. This view came into office with President Reagan. It was expressed in the president's mandate to close the ICBM window, although most of the specific programs for closing it—notably, the Trident SLBM with the D-5 warhead, the air-launched cruise missiles (ALCMs) and submarine-launched cruise missiles (SLCMs), the MX, and the "stealth" bomber (invisible to radar)—were launched by the Carter administration.

Another mark of the failure of SALT to fulfill its expectations, although the correlation was less direct, was the Soviet proliferation of the medium-range SS-20 missiles and the NATO decision, in response, to deploy 572 intermediate-range missiles (the Pershing II and cruise missiles) in Western Europe. Because SALT restricted only "strategic" missiles, the Soviets were free to deploy hundreds of medium-range missiles—the mobile, three-warhead SS-20—and to gain a monopoly of medium-range missiles in Europe. Partly to prevent this monopoly but, basically, to answer German Chancellor Helmut Schmidt's call for a visible means of coupling the United States' strategic weapons to the defense of Europe (a call stimulated by his suspicion that President Carter might make a deal in SALT to ban cruise missiles in order to get limits on strategic weapons), the United States reluctantly accepted. For the sake of allied solidarity in the face of the intensive Soviet campaign against INF, however, the United States soon became the champion of NATO's decision to deploy INF. Then, surprisingly, inter-mediate-range missiles became the target of a burgeoning European antinuclear movement. Although the deployment decision was motivated more by the politics of reassuring the allies about extended deterrence than by technical military requirements, it was (no less than efforts to close the window of vulnerability) a reaction to the Soviet exploitation of SALT, which marked the shattering of hopes for arms control as the primary instrument of East-West stability.

Minimalist defenders of SALT I and II argued, not unrea-sonably, that the intensity of the arms competition would have been greater without these agreements and that the decision of both sides not to undercut the provisions of the unratified SALT II treaty demonstrated their utility. They argued that it was not the concept of stabilizing the existing rough parity of forces that was at fault but the failure of either side to foresee the importance of extending the implementation of the concept to include a ban, or deep-cut limit, on MIRVs.

Be that as it may, the fact of the matter was that the SALT agreements failed to confirm even the most modest claim that the Cambridge school made for strategic arms control: that it would moderate and make more predictable the arms com-petition. Surely the agreements had not improved East-West relations. In their maximalist critics' eyes, the most serious shortcoming of these agreements was that they failed to reduce the risk of war by stabilizing the military balance against the possibility of a nuclear first-strike. Instead, the critics declared, MIRVing made both sides more vulnerable to nuclear first-strikes by increasing the ratio of warheads to missiles and aim points, thereby making ICBMs more attractive targets. Worse than that, MIRVs combined with superior Soviet throwweight ICBMs gutted the U.S. counterforce retaliatory capability. In these conclusions lay the seeds of the revival of the ABM debate. The maximialists took the lead in promoting the old Safeguard rationale based now on much more effective BMD technology, and the minimalists contended that revival of BMD deployments would undermine the stability of the nuclear balance, precipitate a provocative arms race, and cause a dangerous and costly militarization of space.

The not-illogical reaction of some minimalists to the window of vulnerability was to abandon the land-based leg of the strategic triad and concentrate on developing the air and sea legs, supplemented by cruise missiles (SLCMs and GLCMs). Opposition to the Sentinel system had been based on the infeasibility and undesirability of trying to defend cities. Many scientists and others who opposed an area defense were not opposed to protecting missiles. But by the 1980s the opposition to, like the support for, strategic defense had shifted its focus to missile-defense weapons. Then the leading argument put forth by some minimalists came to be that abandoning the ABM Treaty would destroy all hope of reducing or even stabilizing strategic forces by touching off a wide-ranging offensive/defensive arms race, which would only enable the USSR to improve its strategic position.

Among civilian strategists, however, the more influential reaction to the post-SALT shift in the ICBM balance was the one represented by the Scowcroft Commission. After it became clear that deceptive basing modes, such as the extensive "race track" system that would have been deployed in Utah and Nevada, were politically unacceptable, the Scowcroft Commission in April 1983 recommended moving toward mobile single-warhead missiles, such as the prospective Midgetman. It also recommended the deployment of 100 MIRVed MX missiles in hard silos, partly for bargaining leverage with the Soviets and partly to gain a consensus for the report.

However, implementation of the commission's report ran afoul of budgetary stringencies. Congress limited the number of authorized MXs to fifty. The future of the Midgetman was darkened by the great cost per unit and by uncertainties about whether two or more warheads should be placed on it in order to get more firepower for the money. Consequently, in the 1980s it became increasingly doubtful that a politically and economically acceptable mode of protecting U.S. ICBMs could be found—unless BMD came to the rescue.

To the maximalists, the political and economic constraints against reducing the vulnerability of ICBMs by changing their technology and basing mode made the legal constraints accepted in the ABM Treaty seem all the more obsolete and the new conventional BMD technology that had been developed since the treaty all the more attractive as a method of restoring the viability of the land-based leg of the strategic triad. In the maximalist view of the late 1970s, modernized short- and long-range ABMs, with improved radars and sensors, might yet prove to be the most—perhaps the only—cost-effective measures for protecting fixed military sites (including C^3I) by the 1990s.

As Reagan came into office in 1980, old ABM opponents were claiming that the growing vulnerability of U.S. ICBMs confirmed their warnings about the adverse effect of SALT on the strategic balance and that these adversities could not be reversed simply by investing more in strategic forces. What was urgently needed, they argued, was a reappraisal of the ABM Treaty in light of its failure to stabilize the strategic balance. They hoped to restore the survivability of the land-based leg of the strategic triad by utilizing the new technology for interception ballistic missiles in their boost-phase, exo-atmospheric phase, and terminal phase with integrated layers of nonnuclear (including, eventually, directed-energy and other exotic BMD) weapons.[55]

REAGAN'S REVIVAL OF ARMS CONTROL

There were good reasons to think that the Reagan administration, upon assuming office in 1980, would become the champion of the pro-ABM forces. Strongly critical of the strategic arms agreements and coming to power with a mandate to restore U.S. nuclear strength, the administration was the haven and hope for leading maximalists. It came into office deploring the whole process of arms control as previously conducted and resolved not to resume the process until the military balance had been restored and there was evidence of Soviet good behavior in the Third World and elsewhere. Nevertheless, President Reagan soon turned his great popular appeal and political skill toward making arms control the centerpiece of East-West relations. Not only that; by making arms control the instrument of a radical restructuring of deterrence on a nonnuclear basis, he gave it a greatly expanded role, rivaling the role of disarmament in the Baruch Plan and in the subsequent formula of General and Complete Disarmament, which dominated the East-West competition in utopias during the 1950s. Yet, seemingly, he achieved this revival and expansion of arms control with the general approval of the maximalists. Even more remarkable, he prescribed that adherence to the ABM Treaty, not its abrogation or revision, should be the basis for negotiating arms reductions, even though the ultimate objective of such reductions would require the deployment of strategic defense systems prohibited by this treaty, and the function of such systems was a more far-reaching protection of people than ABM advocates had ever imagined.

Reagan's revival of arms control began when the new administration inherited the position of its predecessor on the deployment of INF missiles in Europe. The United States and its European allies, in accordance with the "two-track" approach, had already firmly linked INF deployment with arms negotiations ostensibly intended to reach an East-West agreement on the elimination or limitation of deployments, on the assumption that European publics and parliaments would not accept the deployment without the negotiations to avoid it. Inevitably, this approach to the INF issue put the Reagan administration in the position of championing arms control. Moreover, in the course of championing it, as part of the effort to disarm the rising antideployment forces, the administration proved to be a worthy contender for the highest moral ground by means of the most radical proposal. In the famous "zero" option, it proposed what was, in effect, a radical disarmament treaty for the elimination of all medium-range missiles in Europe and throughout the world, although it did so with full and well-placed confidence that the Soviets (who, alone, had deployed such missiles) would reject the proposal.

INF negotiations, however, soon became a sideshow after the first Pershing IIs were successfully installed in West Germany in 1984 and the heterogeneous peace movement quickly lost its mobilizing rationale. Then the second wave of Reagan's revival of arms control came to the forefront: the commitment to deep reductions of strategic nuclear offensive weapons, symbolized by the "R" in START as the alternative to SALT, which stood condemned for only putting ceilings on existing programs.

The antecedents of START lie in Senator Henry Jackson's attack on SALT on the grounds that it merely sanctioned the arms race. The Cambridge school had denied any necessary correlation between reductions and stability. Indeed, it had reasoned that reductions were likely to be destabilizing, because they would magnify the advantage that one side or the other might gain from quantitative or qualitative improvements. But this position ran contrary to the broad appeal of reductions, from political Left to Right, based on the simple proposition (borrowed from the rationale of disarmament) that since nuclear weapons are dangerous, the fewer there are, the safer we shall all be. The popularity of this approach is attested by the Soviets' adoption, under General Secretary Gorbachev, of the goal of warhead reductions as the means of curbing the arms race and as a step toward eliminating all nuclear weapons.

Government authorities and defense experts have no illusion that reductions are good in themselves. For them the objective is only to get the right kind of reductions—namely, those that reduce the vulnerability of land-based missiles (especially U.S. ICBMs) to the adversary's first-strike capability by reducing the ratio of warheads (especially Soviet warheads) to launchers and aim points. This is the maximalists' formula for reducing the risk of war, as argued most forcefully by Paul Nitze and as incorporated in the Scowcroft Commission Report. But this sophisticated strategic reasoning is absent from both the popular maximalist condemnation of SALT, on the grounds that it was not "real" arms control, and the maximalist advocacy of reductions as the only way to curb the nuclear danger.

The popular maximalist position coincides with the minimalist fondness for reductions, but the latter springs from quite different strategic premises. From the minimalists' standpoint, the comparative numbers of warheads and the ratio of warheads to targets are irrelevant as long as the absolute numbers are so large that either side could meet a first strike with hundreds of retaliatory strikes. The objectives of reductions, in this view, should be to curb the arms race, not to stabilize a balance based on the illusion that comparative warfighting capabilities make a difference.[56]

In spite of their popular appeal, nuclear reductions make the achievement of arms control more difficult. Military establishments are reluctant to give up important weapons that represent considerable investment of resources and planning. In addition, the deeper the reductions, the more difficult it becomes for armed adversaries to agree on the precise numbers and categories of weapons, since reductions inevitably impinge more drastically upon existing programs and deployments and upon the total relationship of forces than do codifications of the existing relationship of forces. This difficulty is compounded by the current asymmetries of strategic force structures, with the Soviets depending far more on MIRVed ICBMs and the United States more on SLBMs, bombers, and cruise missiles. Nevertheless, the Reagan administration has succeeded, far beyond the capacity of antinuclear groups, in making reductions the indispensable test of true arms control.

At the same time, it has managed simultaneously to keep the ABM treaty as the foundation of arms control (while pronouncing SALT II obsolete) and to declare its commitment to a vast strategic defense program. Thus, in arms talks the United States endorses the popular position that arms reductions must be contingent on adherence to the ABM Treaty, while demanding that Moscow, which has undoubtedly violated it by constructing the ABM housing at Krasnoyarsk, comply with the treaty. The more the United States demands compliance with the ABM Treaty, the more committed it becomes to retaining the treaty. Yet, as long as the United States makes adherence to the ABM Treaty a principal component of its arms control position, the Soviets will have little or no incentive to concede the kind of trade-offs that the United States wants in order to diminish the threat of SS-18s and SS-19s to its ICBMs. The reason is that, with or without the constraints of SALT II, the ABM Treaty restrictions on strategic defense assure the Soviets a quantitative advantage in counterforce hard-target kill capabilities. Thus, adherence to the ABM

Treaty, like nuclear offensive reductions, impedes the achievement of the kind of arms agreement that would serve maximalist
strategic goals, while nevertheless providing the foundation for
the revival of arms control.

The ABM Treaty, however, is not easy to abandon or change.
It stands as the only ratified achievement—and a treaty of
unlimited duration, at that—of strategic arms negotiations. It
is widely regarded at home and abroad as the linchpin of East-
West peace, which, if removed, would precipitate a dangerously
destabilizing arms race. A mark of its sacrosanct status is that
the Reagan administration swears to observe the ABM Treaty—
and in its restrictive interpretation (although the administration
denies the legality of this interpretation)—as the condition of
negotiating offensive nuclear reductions, even though the treaty
prohibits the implementation of Reagan's strategic defense
program, upon which the administration is spending tens of
billions of dollars.

If the U.S. government should decide that it needs to revise
or withdraw from the ABM Treaty, whether in order to protect
ICBMs or national populations, or simply to gain some bargaining leverage in arms negotiations that it otherwise badly
lacks, either action could arouse substantial opposition in the
United States and Europe. This opposition would not be allayed
(indeed, it might be further provoked) if the United States
sought the legalistic way out of its dilemma—that is, by
selectively abandoning the restrictive interpretation of the ABM
Treaty through "proportionate responses" to Soviet noncompliance. On the other hand, if the United States continues to
adhere to the ABM Treaty restrictions while the Soviets reject
the kind of offensive reductions the United States wants and
further increase their advantage in nuclear striking power,
substantial opposition will be awakened among American critics
of SALT and proponents of redressing the nuclear balance.
Either way, the ABM Treaty could become the focus of a
renewed debate between minimalists and maximalists—unless
the United States can formulate a negotiable arms control
position that substantially reduces nuclear warheads and SS-
18 warheads in particular.

During Reagan's term of office, however, the latent ABM debate was virtually foreclosed, not only by the administration's incorporation of the treaty in a popular arms control proposal that envisaged deep reductions but also by Reagan's proclamation of the strategic defense initiative (SDI), which subordinated the role of terminal-defense ABMs to the much more ambitious goal of a layered defense—against missiles in boost phase and midphase as well as in terminal phase—in order to protect national populations and abolish the dependence of mutual East-West deterrence on nuclear retaliation. SDI, moreover, not only preempted the revival of the pro-ABM campaign; it also completed the Reagan administration's revival of arms control as the centerpiece of East-West relations. On the one hand, as it became impossible to imagine the restructuring of deterrence without Soviet agreement to constrain offense-defense competition, SDI required the most comprehensive, instrusive, and radical role for arms control since the concept of arms control replaced disarmament in the early 1960s. On the other hand, the Soviet Union portrayed SDI as the sole obstacle to the achievement of arms control and defined the ultimate goal of arms control in terms of complete nuclear disarmament. SDI and arms control, therefore, became the most contentious and emotion-laden issues in East-West relations, inexorably linked with each other in a package of military concerns that would greatly agitate old controversies surrounding the nuclear dilemma throughout the 1980s at the least.

5

The New Strategic Debate

In preempting the emerging ABM debate and helping to place comprehensive arms control at the center of East-West relations, SDI became a kind of bridge between the opposing extremes of a wider controversy over how to deal with the nuclear dilemma, with warwinning maximalists on one side and theological or philosophical abolitionists on the other. These two extremes were both stimulated by the disillusionment with arms control that accompanied the collapse of détente. SDI, whether by calculation or intuition, was a response to both.

SDI, in theory, might resolve a mounting challenge to the strategic consensus of the 1960s and 1970s from the maximalists, at one end of the spectrum, and the abolitionists, at the other, by transcending both positions through a restructuring of deterrence on a nonnuclear basis. Soon after Reagan's initiative, however, it was clear that SDI was anathema to the abolitionists and that it attracted no support from the minimalists. Only among the maximalists did it gain significant support, either as a surrogate for ABMs or as a means of funding ABMs. In practical terms this support encountered mounting technological and budgetary obstacles, not to mention strong opposition to the basic rationale of SDI in Congress and in Western Europe. But regardless of the fate of SDI, the elements of a new debate on strategic defense were gathering in the deepening controversy between the opponents of MAD and the opponents of counterforce strategy, of which the incipient ABM debate of the late 1970s was only one manifestation.

On the right were the maximalists, who were calling not merely for the restoration of some of the lost invulnerability of U.S. land-based retaliatory forces but also for the revival of a longer-lost capacity to win a counterforce war (or at least end it on favorable terms). They attributed most of the global adversities of the 1970s to the U.S. loss and the Soviet gain of strategic superiority—to the Soviet drive beyond strategic parity; the Soviet deployments of hundreds of SS-20s in Europe; the rise of the antinuclear movement and of European "neutralism" and "appeasement"; the Soviet expansion of influence in the Third World, from Angola to Vietnam; and the Soviet threat to the Gulf, following the collapse of the shah's Iran and the Soviet invasion of Afghanistan. They called for the restoration of U.S. qualitative nuclear superiority, not only to close the window of vulnerability but also to acquire an advantageous warfighting capability.

The exemplar of this new wave of maximalist strategists who attracted the most attention abroad as well as at home was Colin Gray, whose advocacy of flexible and controlled nuclear responses differed from official doctrine principally in its lack of nuances. In a controversial article he co-authored in 1980—"Victory Is Possible"[57]—Gray deplored U.S. reliance upon strategic parity and MAD for deterrence, charging that this posture was not only an incredible bluff (especially as applied to extended deterrence) but also an immoral strategy because it was contrary to the guidelines of the doctrine of just war. Instead, he advocated that the United States plan its nuclear posture in order to defeat the Soviet Union, at a cost that would not prohibit U.S. recovery, by a combination of counterforce offensive targeting, civil defense, and ballistic missile and air defense. One especially controversial component of this strategy was decapitation—the capacity to destroy Soviet political leadership and bureaucracy in Moscow with precise nuclear strikes—which differed from PD-59 only in the absence of the qualification that it should be only a last resort in an all-out war.

In muted form, this maximalist counterattack against MAD found an official voice during the Reagan administration, when a host of members of the Committee on the Present Danger gained positions in the White House (Richard Pipes), State Department (Paul Nitze), Defense Department (Richard Perle, Fred Ikle, Andrew Marshall, T. K. Jones), ACDA (Eugene Rostow), and the president's Foreign Intelligence Advisory Board (Edward Teller). Rejecting the dominant assumption since the ABM Treaty that deterrence could or should be based on Soviet acceptance of mutual assured vulnerability, the newly installed maximalists vowed that the United States must beat the Soviets at their own game of counterforce warfighting. This approach was represented most conspicuously in the Department of Defense's first comprehensive "Defense Guidance," produced in the spring of 1982, which explicitly called for plans to defeat the Soviet Union at any level of conflict and to "prevail" even in a "protracted" nuclear war with the Soviet Union.[58]

The *New York Times* got news of the word "prevail," which critics interpreted to mean "achieve victory." In response to the alarmed opposition to a warwinning strategy, Secretary of Defense Weinberger denied that the government believed that either side could win a nuclear war; it was only determined to deny victory to the USSR. Subsequent revisions of the formulation in his annual reports to the Congress, to the effect that the United States must seek termination of a major war on terms favorable to the United States and its allies, further distanced the Department of Defense's rhetoric from that of Colin Gray.[59] By 1985 President Reagan's oft-repeated admonition that "a nuclear war cannot be won and must not be fought" had become a ubiquitous axiom of official pronouncements about nuclear policy. Whether or not these qualified reformulations changed operational plans (which is doubtful), they foreshadowed more significant rhetorical concessions to, or co-options of, antinuclear positions that had captured the headlines during the INF deployment crisis.

On the left, the minimalists were on the defensive. They generally denied the accusation that they advocated MAD insofar as it was identified with finite deterrence, but they

were nevertheless obliged to defend MAD as the central,
existential reality of deterrence in the nuclear age. Spurgeon
Keeny and Wolfgang Panofsky counterattacked by defending
MAD as existential deterrence and labeling the ascendant
school of counterforce as NUTS (for Nuclear Utilization Target
Selection).[60] The MAD world, they argued, is inescapable
because it is "inherent in the tremendous power of nuclear
weapons, the size of nuclear stockpiles, the collateral damage
associated with the use of nuclear weapons against military
targets, the technical limitations on strategic area defense, and
the uncertainties involved in efforts to control the escalation
of nuclear war." Good strategic sense, they concluded, requires
accepting the existence of MAD but making it more stable
and less dangerous.

Few minimalists, however, rose to the defense of MAD on
these or any other grounds. The minimalists' trouble at the
outset of the Reagan administration was that they were on
the wrong side of the revitalization of containment. Discredited
by the failure of limited war in Vietnam—most conspicuously,
the failure of selective bombing as a form of coercive bargaining
in the Rolling Thunder campaign—and by the failure of arms
control in the collapse of détente and the abortion of SALT
II, they needed an appealing program or policy position in
order to remobilize. For a brief period in 1982 and 1983, it
seemed that the minimalists might find a surrogate for SALT
in the nuclear freeze movement, which attracted a broad
coalition of those opposed to what were regarded as the Reagan
administration's bellicose policies and rhetoric. But the nuclear
freeze, which originated among left-wing and pacifist critics
of containment, was never much more than a symbol of anxiety
about nuclear weapons. Insofar as the movement's originators
had a military strategy, it was hard to distinguish from finite
deterrence as it displayed an acute allergy to counterforce and
limited-war strategies and to missiles regarded as provocative
first-strike weapons (especially the MX).[61] When the freeze
movement suddenly expanded to phenomenal dimensions in
the spring of 1982, it became an all-encompassing cause; joined
by a broad spectrum of mitigators and all sorts of concerned
citizens and politicians, it consequently lost whatever coherence

it had initially held. When in the spring of 1983 Congress tried to turn the symbol of a freeze into a resolution embodying specific recommendations concerning military and arms control policies, the cause suffered a fatal exposure to its intrinsic ambiguity and to the conflicting prescriptions of its supporters. It survived only as a plank in the Democratic platform of 1984. President Reagan's victory and his continuing support of comprehensive arms negotiations as a parallel "track" to the INF deployment program ended the challenge the concept of nuclear freeze made to the prevailing strategic consensus. But it left the field of opposition open to the abolitionists.

THE RESURGENCE OF ABOLITIONISM

In the 1980s the abolitionist approach gained favor in proportion to the fading of hopes for either a strategic arms agreement or a freeze. The major catalyst for the resurgence of abolition was the organized opposition to INF deployments in Europe: the sudden ascendance of a surprisingly active and politically ambitious (though politically naive and, in the end, ineffectual) antinuclear (or, as self-styled, "peace") movement, which teamed conventional antimilitarist groups with ecologists and countercultural cadres. But it was the churches that provided the major organized intellectual leadership for the renunciation of nuclear deterrence. They were aided and abetted by those military commentators and analysts who dissected in detail the deficiencies of the command and control of nuclear exchanges, and by the scientists who warned that nuclear exchanges would lead to a global ecological disaster (called "nuclear winter") long before the superpowers would have exhausted their nuclear arsenals.[62]

Against the background of European antinuclear protest and the freeze movement, the American Catholic bishops, through intensive hearings and discussions and three draft reports, finally voted approval in May 1983 of a pastoral letter, *The Challenge of Peace,* which gained great publicity among laypersons as well as clergy of Protestant denominations.[63] The letter's central message was the familiar injunction to "say 'no' to nuclear war" on the principal grounds that any use of nuclear weapons is bound to lead to such unconscionable destruction as to be beyond justification for any political purpose. In translating this message into policy, however, the letter stopped short of counseling an absolute "no" to nuclear *deterrence,* except for deterrence based on nuclear first-use. Reflecting the protracted process of compromise and consensus-building from which it derived, *The Challenge of Peace* absolutely condemned the first-use of nuclear weapons. It endorsed the policy of moving toward an adequate nonnuclear defense posture in Europe in order to sustain extended deterrence, but found no merit in the hope that nuclear escalation or limited nuclear options might limit damage to morally tolerable levels. In proscribing any use of nuclear force, it also condemned the intention to use nuclear weapons to deter the first-use of nuclear weapons, even if the intention included the avoidance of cities and collateral civil damage. Yet it qualified this condemnation by conferring a "strictly conditional moral acceptance" of retaliatory deterrence if such deterrence were a temporary step on the way toward "progressive disarmament." This conclusion was tantamount to holding that the nuclear dilemma is morally unacceptable and can only temporarily be mitigated by moving toward the abolition of nuclear weapons. At the same time, however, the letter stopped short of explicitly endorsing the concept of a nonnuclear world.

The ecumenical appeal of this qualified abolitionism was later manifested in the unqualified condemnation of nuclear weapons contained in the pastoral letter of the United Methodists, released in April 1986. Also based on extensive hearings and discussions, this letter rejected the Catholic bishops' uneasy compromise with nuclear deterrence. It concluded that nuclear war cannot possibly be compatible with the principles of just war; declared that "nuclear deterrence has become a dogmatic license for perpetual hostility between the superpowers and for their rigid resistance to significant measures of disarmament"; and proclaimed that "the ideology of deterrence must not receive the churches' blessing, even as a temporary warrant for holding on to nuclear weapons." The only thing that could justify the "lingering possession" of nuclear weapons for a "strictly limited time" would be "an ethic of reciprocity," shaped by a "realistic vision of common security and the escalation of mutual trust," as nuclear-weapon states act together, in agreed stages, to eliminate these weapons.[64]

Author Jonathan Schell was equally absolute in his rejection of nuclear deterrence. In his view, moving toward disarmament could not mitigate the moral enormity of nuclear deterrence. In his immensely popular book *The Fate of the Earth,* published in 1982 and initially serialized in the *New Yorker,* he asserted that "we have no choice but to address the issue of nuclear weapons as though we knew for a certainty that their use would put an end to our species;"[65] that sooner or later, as nuclear stockpiles and the accuracy and speed of nuclear weapons increase, deterrence must fail and nuclear war must result; and that salvation lies only in abolishing nuclear weapons under the equivalent of world government.

Two years later, in a second book, *The Abolition* (which attracted far less attention), Schell was no less convinced of civilization's eventual nuclear extinction as long as the superpowers practiced nuclear deterrence. However, he reached the conclusion that world government is as impractical a road to abolition as any of the less radical step-by-step prescriptions of the peace movement, such as deep nuclear reductions, the nuclear freeze, and the renunciation of nuclear first-use. Instead, he proposed a new way of eliminating nuclear weapons while preserving national sovereignty, admittedly inspired by President Reagan's announcement of SDI: basing mutual deterrence, as a first step, on the agreed abolition of offensive nuclear weapons; then, on the retention of limited, balanced conventional "antinuclear defenses" as a hedge against cheating; and, ultimately, on the capacity for nuclear rearmament, rather than on nuclear weapons in being.[66]

THE STRATEGIC DEFENSE INITIATIVE

President Reagan's enunciation of SDI on March 23, 1983, was a response (whether calculated or not) to both the maximalists' and the abolitionists' criticism of the pragmatic strategic consensus—a consensus that had been weakened by the collapse of détente, the abortion of SALT, and the resurgence of the peace movement. It was a response that transcended the extremities as well as the maximalist/minimalist center of the spectrum of approaches toward the nuclear dilemma. In coupling the abolitionist end to maximalist means, it also linked an extraordinarily ambitious military program to the pursuit of an extremely comprehensive arms agreement.

SDI, Reagan has declared, is a research program aimed at achieving a full-scale layered strategic defense system, extended to Western Europe and reciprocated by the Soviet Union, that will so effectively protect national populations from nuclear attack as to make nuclear weapons "impotent and obsolete." The president did not say whether this ultimate goal—let us call it the Defended World—was to be attained in the natural course of unrestricted competition or through an arms agreement, but subsequent pronouncements confirmed what common sense clearly indicates: In order to achieve the Defended World and sustain it, it will have to be created by controlled stages of disarmament and guaranteed by a comprehensive arms agreement. Thus, official pronouncements prescribed that the way to get from the Undefended to the Defended World is by means of "cooperative" measures—that is, through transitional arms agreements.

The first prescribed step, although not visionary, would be difficult enough to achieve. It is to stabilize, not transform, the existing structure of deterrence through an agreement to get deep reductions of nuclear warheads. The purpose of these reductions would be to reduce the vulnerability of ICBMs and their C^3I facilities to the threat of a sudden first-strike against hardened ICBMs. And the reductions would be achieved while strictly adhering to the ABM Treaty (despite the government's much less restrictive legal interpretation of what the treaty permits in the development and testing of weapons and components based on "other physical principles"). But this first phase would also have to lead to the last. Therefore, it would hold open the option of implementing SDI if research showed that the weapons were sufficiently "lethal, survivable, and cost-effective at the margin" (in Nitze's words) to produce an advantageous ratio of the U.S. capacity to destroy incoming missiles to the Soviet capacity to penetrate U.S. defenses. To offset Soviet concerns that SDI deployments would facilitate a U.S. first-strike by shielding the United States against Soviet retaliation, Reagan proposed at Reykjavik, in November 1986, that all ballistic nuclear weapons be eliminated in ten years, prior to any deployment of strategic defense weapons. In an even more radical commitment to the abolitionist goal, he repeatedly insisted that the population shields must be mutual; accordingly, he promised to share with the Soviet Union the benefits of SDI technology when it becomes operational.

Thus, SDI is an odd marriage of the abolitionist goal with a maximalist defense program, guaranteed by a comprehensive arms agreement. It promises adherence to the ABM Treaty— at least until the decision to deploy SDI weapons can be made and as long as there is a prospect of gaining deep nuclear reductions—in order to achieve the long-term transformation of the basis of deterrence from mutual assured destruction to mutual assured defense. It postulates strategic defense systems capable of achieving deterrence by means of near-perfect nonnuclear denial capabilities. In this repsect, despite its linkage to a far-reaching arms agreement, SDI is a consummation of the ultimate maximalist goal of relieving deterrence of both the uncertainties of mutual mind reading and the uncertain tests of national resolve by basing deterrence on effective defensive warfighting capabilities under unilateral national control. The strategy for achieving the Defended World postpones all the hard choices that are required to integrate this goal with arms control policy into a strategy of action by insisting that SDI is, as yet, only a research program. But it also argues against conceding any restrictions on the development and testing of SDI components that go beyond the official interpretation of the ABM Treaty (which, even in its restrictive form, is much broader than the Soviet interpretation) on the grounds that using SDI as a bargaining chip in return for nuclear reductions (even for a limited period of years) would kill the prospect of achieving the ultimate goal.

Will SDI succeed in bridging the gap between abolitionism and maximalism? Will it fuse and mobilize the support of the maximalists and minimalists so as to become the basis of a new strategic consensus sustained by arms control? The prospect is exceedingly unlikely. The more probable outcome, if the U.S. government continues to define SDI in terms of Reagan's ultimate goal, is that SDI will lead to a stalemate in arms negotiations and a revival of the debate between maximalists and minimalists. In that case, the debate would revolve around the contradiction between the ABM Treaty and the restoration of a less vulnerable, more lethal warfighting capability—a debate in which the objective of protecting national populations would be distinctly subordinate to the prospect of protecting missiles. The now-hidden but widely believed premise underlying this ironic fate of SDI is, simply, that its ultimate goal is impossible to achieve and, under any realistic conditions, probably undesirable if it could be achieved. This point has not escaped the notice of the mitigators, but few of them have chosen to say publicly that the king has no clothes on when the enormity of the pretense promises to extract from the fanciful wardrobe of abolition some added protection against the nakedness of MAD. Therefore, an open controversy over the practical implications of SDI for defense programs and arms control may not take place until SDI, in a post-Reagan regime, becomes more like a normal set of defense programs than a utopian goal and until these programs become integrated with a truly negotiable arms control proposal.

To understand these harsh judgments, one need only appreciate the basic conditions for creating and sustaining the Defended World. These conditions go beyond technological and economic feasibility. The peace of this world would have to depend on a stable military equilibrium that deterred both sides from either seeking a decisive military advantage or avoiding a decisive disadvantage by means of attack. The stability of this equilibrium would have to depend on the stability of an effective nonnuclear balance, on the efficacy and stability of deterrence based on the prospect of nuclear rearmament, and on the effectiveness and reliability of the arms-control regime. None of these three conditions, let alone all three together, is practicable.

The kind of conventional balance in Europe against Warsaw Pact forces that could substitute nonnuclear for nuclear deterrents may hypothetically be feasible, but there is no reason to believe that the very real domestic burdens that such a posture must entail would be politically and economically acceptable to any of the allies—or to the United States, for that matter—in return for the hypothetical benefits of the Defended World. In fact, the European governments, convinced that nuclear deterrence is primarily responsible for the unprecedented decades of peace they have enjoyed since World War II, regard a nonnuclear military balance, if it could be achieved, as a fatal threat to deterrence. In a nonnuclear world the threat of nuclear rearmament might constitute a deterrent to aggression, but in European eyes it would be no substitute for nuclear weapons in existence; and, as there would be a premium on rapid rearmament and a decisive first strike, such a threat would be highly destabilizing.

An effective and reliable arms control regime intended to maintain a stable nonnuclear, defense-dominant structure of deterrence would have to be far more comprehensive and intrusive—yet much more adaptable to ever-advancing technology—than any strategic arms agreement yet envisaged. It would have to guarantee that, despite the rapid rate of technological innovation and the opportunities for cheating, not only strategic ballistic missiles but all kinds of offensive nuclear weapons and counter-defensive weapons would remain impotent and obsolete. It would have to guarantee that anti-offensive weapons would not threaten the space-based sensors and battle-management computers necessary for strategic and tactical defense, and that constant improvements in space-based defense weapons would not give these weapons an offensive capability. The problems of reliable verification and effective response to evidence of Soviet noncompliance would be many orders of magnitude greater than those with which the United States is currently struggling. Yet any breakdown in the arms control regime would jeopardize the whole structure of mutual deterrence. In short, the Defended World, even if it could be achieved, would be dangerously fragile and ephemeral. But the difficulties of achieving SALT I and II, as well as the deficiencies of these agreements in moderating and stabilizing the arms competition against technological advances for even a decade, strongly indicate that creating the Defended World through arms control is infeasible to begin with. Even if one assumes that the Soviets see a hypothetical military interest in a structure of mutual deterrence based on the dominance of conventional defense over the nuclear offense—an interest that runs directly contrary to their commitment to the "ceaseless dialectic" between offensive and defensive weapons—there is no basis for believing that the United States and the USSR would embrace the kind of national security cooperation on the grandest scale that would be necessary to achieve the Defended World.

This is not to say that the mitigators must be satisfied forever with a structure of deterrence that depends so heavily on the threat of mutual suicide and the accompanying prospect of a global ecological disaster. Rather, in response to the realities that the abolitionists seek to escape, they are increasingly bound to look for ways to make deterrence stable but, at the same time, less dependent on mutual nuclear vulnerability and less prone to destroy life and the means of livelihood if deterrence fails. SDI, by concentrating attention on the objective of impenetrable population shields and the obsolescence of nuclear weapons, has skewed consideration of the role of strategic defense and nuclear deterrence by representing it as an all-or-nothing choice. Consequently, the current debate about strategic defense has paid little attention to the value of either partial population defense or reduced dependence on nuclear retaliatory deterrence, both of which were objectives of the earliest advocates of an ABM program.

STRATEGIC DEFENSE IN THE REAL WORLD ————————————————

East-West Equilibrium

It is not written in the nature of the cold war or the dynamics of military competition that the East-West military balance should forever be exclusively dependent on offensive nuclear weapons while the defenses against them are kept impotent by mutual agreement. Given the greatly enhanced effectiveness of strategic defense technology since the ABM Treaty, there may be promise of practical significance in a defense-reliant structure of deterrence that would destroy 70 or only 50 percent of incoming missiles—even though a structure intended to destroy nearly 100 percent is unrealistic. In such a Partially Defended World, some nuclear weapons would remain a tangible reminder of the awful potential of nuclear destruction. However, they would be reduced to a level at which they would be functionally obsolete as counterforce warfighting weapons, leaving nonnuclear defensive capabilities as the primary deterrent to the first-use of nuclear weapons. If nuclear weapons were used nevertheless, there would be a compelling incentive to use them only as bargaining measures to terminate the war; and the prospect that nuclear bargaining would lead to nuclear winter would be greatly diminished by their limited number. Thus, the physical basis for strategies that were first articulated a quarter-century ago and that still appeal to a broad spectrum of mitigators might emerge from the operationally significant residue of SDI abolitionism.

Time may show that the technological developments taking place now (such as the substitution of conventional for tactical and even strategic nuclear weapons) will make a 70 percent East-West defense practicable.[67] Such developments may even make the achievement of this transformed structure of deterrence feasible without an unrealistically comprehensive, flexible, and intrusive arms control regime. In fact, even in the absence of formal arms constraints, an unencumbered competition between offensive and defensive weapons over a decade or two would probably produce a more defense-reliant equilibrium; and the wide variety of new and interdependent weapons upon which this equilibrium would be based, considering the enormous uncertainties it would pose for any government contemplating a first strike, would not necessarily produce a military structure any less stable than the present equilibrium, which does not depend much on formal arms constraints either. But speculation about a Partially Defended World, with or without a comprehensive framework of arms control to guarantee it, is much too conjectural in the 1980s to lead to any definite policy conclusion—except that the United States should keep open the option to achieve it until much more is known about whether it may be technologically, economically, and politically feasible.

In the meantime, there are problems enough in coping with the proximate objective of integrating military policies, arms reductions, and the ABM Treaty in such a way as to stabilize the existing structure of deterrence, based on the inescapable risk of mutual assured destruction. These problems are rife with possibilities for a resurgence of debate between the minimalists and the maximalists. If mitigation fails to produce results—especially in arms control—the abolitionists will hail this failure as confirmation that only Utopia can save us from Armageddon.

The prospect of such a failure arises from the fact that the Soviets have no incentive to limit offensive systems in which they hold a quantitative lead so long as the United States holds open the option of deploying SDI, a technology in which they are inferior. At least they have no incentive so long as the United States is constrained from actually deploying or threatening to deploy SDI by its adherence to the ABM Treaty. For even if the United States finally decides to exceed the SALT II limits, which it has declared obsolete because of Soviet violations, the Soviet Union will retain and probably increase its quantitative superiority in strategic strike forces. Therefore, only the fear of open, unconstrained competition across the broad spectrum of advanced SDI technology gives Moscow an incentive to concede constraints on Soviet offensive missiles in order to curb this threat. But by holding the United States to the terms of the ABM Treaty and representing SDI as the sole obstacle to radical arms reductions, Moscow hopes to gain through public diplomacy and propaganda the desired constraints against SDI without paying anything for them in an arms bargain.

Under these conditions, U.S. ICBMs will become increasingly vulnerable (because of the political and economic constraints on all means of reducing their vulnerability, including the deployment of ABMs) as the USSR increases its lead in prompt hard-target kill capabilities and reduces the vulnerability of its strategic force by deploying mobile single-warhead and MIRVed missiles, building up its force of ALCMs (cruise missiles launched from bombers), putting more ballistic and cruise missiles at sea, and developing the potential for an ABM and ATBM (antitactical ballistic missile) breakout. Consequently, if the United States wishes to have a viable land-based strategic force, it will eventually either have to cut an arms deal that will secure the kind of offensive strategic reductions it needs to close the window of vulnerability, in return for some constraints on the SDI program, or it will have to consider unilaterally deploying parts of SDI in violation of the ABM Treaty if and as they become operational and cost-effective. If the present arms negotiation stalemate drags on and the U.S. strategic position worsens, the United States will be under growing pressure to pursue both courses. Their respective advocates among the minimalists and maximalists will reiterate the previous ABM debates, but this time they will do so against the background of a more powerful abolitionist coalition and a more restive, assertive allied opinion in Europe.

The European Dimension

The European dimension of the debate will be more prominent for four reasons:

1. Europeans are anxious to see arms control progress in order to suppress the Soviet threat and promote East-West détente.
2. Europeans are concerned that SDI, which implies a nonnuclear Europe and is incompatible with the British and French nuclear forces, will be an obstacle to an arms agreement.
3. The Soviet proposal for an INF agreement would eliminate the European medium-range missiles in the first stage toward eliminating all nuclear weapons and so raise the fear of decoupling that INF was deployed to allay. The United States is disposed to accept some such deal as the easiest way to get an arms agreement, as evidenced

by President Reagan's proposal for zero medium-range missiles in Europe and Asia and the subsequent elimination of all ballistic nuclear weapons in ten years. Although allied governments will certainly warn the United States against pursuing any such agreement (if only by insisting that it must be postulated on the achievement of an adequate conventional balance, preferably by arms control), and the United States will be inclined to heed their warning, the prospect that the vision of denuclearization will prove irresistible cannot be dismissed.

4. ATBMs may emerge as a major issue. The Soviets have already deployed a first-generation SA-X-12, whereas NATO has none. Although not prohibited by the ABM Treaty, ATBMs may seem to be a counterpart to SDI, not only because they are hard to distinguish from ABMs but also because Germans and Americans, for different political reasons, may wish to link the two. This linkage may raise questions of conventional defense and arms control that are divisive in European domestic politics.

One can think of ways to head off a possibly corrosive intra-European and U.S.-European controversy on these START and INF-reduction issues, although none is easy. What is required is a negotiable arms-agreement package that simultaneously would meet the need for stabilizing the strategic nuclear balance at a reduced level (say, by 50 percent) in categories of launchers that will diminish reliance on stationary MIRVed ICBMs; hold open but delay for ten years or so implementation of the option to develop, test, and deploy SDI weapons beyond what is permitted by the ABM Treaty in the U.S. restrictive interpretation; limit medium- and short-range missiles at a lower and roughly equal level while preserving enough for coupling; and guard against an ABM circumvention or breakout through ATBMs while not excluding their deployment. Even aside from the SDI problems, however, these objectives, which are impossible to achieve unilaterally, are immensely difficult to achieve cooperatively, given the asymmetrical structures of strategic forces and BMD capabilities, not to mention the problems of ASAT and verification. Nor does this package of arms limitations indicate a resolution of the problem of gaining sufficient carrots or sticks to induce Soviet agreement while observing the constraints of the ABM Treaty.

Seeking an End to the Arms Control Stalemate

In order to persuade the Soviets to accept some such version of the "grand bargain" that optimists envisage, the United States might seek the revision of the ABM Treaty during a specified period of negotiations in order to permit expanded land-based ABM deployments to protect counterforce targets, while extending the ABM Treaty's restrictions on space-based systems for an even longer period. The strategy of such a proposal would be not only to confront the Soviets with a more convincing threat of unilateral SDI deployments if a revision were not agreed to but, at the same time, to draw a distinction between land-based and space-based BMD from which the Soviets would also derive some military gain, because theirs is the only side to have deployed ABMs and they are prepared to extend these deployments. This strategy, however, conflicts with the Reagan administration's commitment to pre-serve the ABM restrictions (and to seek Soviet compliance with them) while negotiating nuclear reductions, its reluctance to accept a revision of the treaty that might give the Soviets a short-run advantage in BMD, and the president's adamant opposition toward any concession to a BMD rationale that falls short of the ultimate SDI goal.

The opening gambits in strategic-force bargaining, set forth by the two heads of state in the summer of 1986, raised great hopes of breaking the arms control stalemate; but these gambits contained substantial differences on offensive as well as defensive restrictions, turning on the magnitude and categories of nuclear warhead reductions and the period and terms of commitment to observe the ABM Treaty. These differences were not over-come at the dramatic October meeting in Reykjavik. There Reagan and Gorbachev apparently agreed to reduce strategic nuclear weapons to 6,000 warheads and 1,600 launchers in five years, but they did not agree to sublimits on SS-18s, which the United States continued to demand. Reagan proposed the elimination of all ballistic nuclear weapons in ten years, to be followed, however, by SDI deployments unless the two sides agreed to extend the ABM Treaty restrictions. Gorbachev proposed to get rid of all nuclear weapons in ten years, but not to permit SDI deployments unless the two sides agreed to revise the ABM Treaty. With respect to INF, Reagan proposed the first-stage elimination of all medium-range missiles in Europe, a limit of 100 in Soviet Asia and the United States, and undefined constraints on short-range missiles, to be followed by the reduction of all ballistic missiles in ten years. Gorbachev seemed to accept the first-stage proposal as a position to bargain about and, before Reykjavik, raised hopes of reaching an INF agreement by announcing that an INF agreement would not be linked to restrictions on SDI and that French and British nuclear forces would not be counted as medium-range missiles in any arms agreement. But at the end of the Reykjavik meeting, he declared that all the Soviet proposals were insep-arable parts of a package in which INF must be included, and he conditioned acceptance of the whole package on an agree-ment to restrict SDI, even to the point of banning research outside "laboratories."

Arms control optimists believed that the exchange of utopias at Reykjavik would impart new momentum toward agreement on the much more limited (approximately 50 percent) reduc-tions that both sides proposed during a first-stage five-year period of negotiations; they were also encouraged by the concessions that both sides (but especially Gorbachev) had made in their first-stage positions. The skeptics, on the other hand, regarded Reykjavik principally as an improvised propaganda contest in which each side sought to capture the moral high ground in order to persuade the American and European publics of the justice of contradictory positions on SDI.

In either case (whether it is the optimists or the skeptics who are correct), if serious bargaining ensues during the tough and protracted negotiations over the details, there will be no quick and sweeping resolution of the dozens of intractable issues that block the way to a mutually satisfactory and reliably verifiable military balance at a substantially reduced level of nuclear forces. And if an actual arms treaty along the lines of the first-stage proposals eventually results, it will call for far less radical changes in the existing East-West military structure and level of forces than the contesting visions at Reykjavik promised.

If the protracted posturing and bargaining fail to demonstrate that agreement (or series of agreements to reconcile strategic defense with nuclear reductions) is feasible, the United States will face the choice of, on the one hand, acquiescing to an indefinite stalemate that concedes the insoluble vulnerability of ICBMs and prohibits any effort to overcome this disadvantage by means of strategic defense or, on the other hand, deciding unilaterally to break out of these constraints or secure an advantageous revision of the ABM Treaty. A respectable case can be made for escaping this predicament by simply accepting the minimalist prescription of a permanently open window of vulnerability—that is, by phasing out the terrestrial leg of the strategic triad—and relying on a triad of modernized cruise missiles (GLCMs, SLCMs, and ALCMs) to supplement SLBMs, IRBMs, and bombers.[68] But no administration is likely to abandon a land-based strategic missile force in the face of a growing Soviet counterforce advantage. Yet, given the commitment to less vulnerable ICBMs, it is as hard to imagine the United States indefinitely accepting the present stalemate as to imagine it unilaterally breaking out of the stalemate. In either case, this predicament is rich with opportunities for the revival of familiar controversies about military strategy and arms control, intensified by the mobilization of a larger security-conscious public by antinuclear activists in both the United States and Western Europe. Inextricably entangled with the issues of strategy and arms control, and accentuated by SDI's problematic bridge between abolition and maximalist mitigation, the familiar moral and ethical issues will loudly resound in the cacophony of controversy.

6

Toward a Concept of
Just Deterrence

It is by following the twists and turns, the contradictions and convolutions, of the American controversies that have revolved around ways of coping with the nuclear dilemma through military strategy and arms control that one can illuminate the complex entanglement of tangible and intangible, calculable and speculative, factors that confound moral and expediential judgment. One may also discover the distortions of oversimplification that these controversies necessarily entail. Yet, in behalf of simplification, it must be said that the distortion of overcomplication is far worse. Any strategic or moral doctrine of just deterrence that purports to refine and elaborate the intrinsic complexity of the myriad of factors and considerations involved into a comprehensive set of guidelines that, when applied to any and every issue, will lead inexorably to a definitive judgment surely imposes a false precision on reality. Perhaps the optimal course of moral reasoning is to take as a baseline the simplifying categories of thought in terms of which the advocates of different positions have actually tried to cope with the nuclear dilemma and appraise them for their guidance in reaching ethical judgments about the major policy issues.

It is as easy to define the basic framework of moral reasoning within which such an appraisal should take place as it is difficult to apply this framework with all the variations and qualifications that sound judgment requires. The framework embodies a relationship between ends (or intentions), means, and consequences such that the moral cost of using, threatening, or planning to use nuclear weapons is not disproportionate to the political purpose, in light of the feasibility of achieving the purpose by the chosen means as compared to alternative means. Or, to put it positively, the framework requires that the overt use of nuclear force or its use as a deterrent must be more likely than any alternative means to achieve a compelling political purpose at a morally acceptable cost.

The application of this framework is difficult because the weight assigned to its three elements—ends, means, and consequences—and the relationship among them are not determinate and fixed but indeterminate and variable. Only those who ascribe an absolute value to the ends (such as survival and deterring or defeating aggression) or to the military means (such as resorting to the first-use of nuclear weapons and avoiding the use or threatened use of nuclear weapons) can simplify this problem intellectually, as only the absolutists can be logically indifferent to the consequences of their policies and actions. But this kind of absolutism is a prescription for moral irresponsibility. For the most compelling end does not justify any and all means, without regard to their moral cost, even if the consequences of the means employed support the end; and if the means, whether costly or benign in moral terms, lead to evil consequences that contradict the intended end, the value of the end will not offset the injustice of failing to implement it in practice. In the real world an absolutist view of ends and means, consistently carried out, would lead to consequences that no one but a fanatic, concerned only with the integrity of his or her principles in the abstract at any cost, could reconcile with morality. Common wisdom tells us that there must be some means that come close to being absolutely prohibited regardless of the consequences and some ends so valuable that almost any means capable of defending them is justified; but any responsible ethical framework must leave these ends and means as undefined exceptions, rather than making them central principles of action.

In the real world, ends or intentions are willed on a broad sliding scale of values from virtuous to evil. The ends themselves are typically multiple and often conflicting. Similarly, the positive or negative value of the means is subject to a great range of moral appraisals, depending on a variety of possible circumstances too diverse to specify in advance. Whether or not the means are effectively related to the ends by the actual consequences of carrying them out is a matter of degree and also a matter of considerable uncertainty and incalculable risk, especially when the use of nuclear weapons is contemplated. Nevertheless, if policies for coping with the nuclear dilemma are to have any force or coherence, they must be generalized and simplified (with due allowance for indispensable exceptions); and the ends-means-consequences framework of moral reasoning must correspondingly be pared to fit the most important and recurrent circumstances, with variations confined to really exceptional and morally significant departures from the norm.

In this spirit of practical moral judgment, let us apply the basic framework of moral reasoning proposed here to the simplifying categories of approach to the nuclear dilemma at the center of U.S. controversies in strategic thought. In these terms, there is no justification, in my view, for the approach of either rejection or abolition in dealing with the nuclear dilemma. The serious moral issues involved call, instead, for the proper mix of maximalist and minimalist approaches.

REJECTION APPRAISED

The warwinning school of rejection manifests an intolerable indifference not only to human suffering, death, and physical and ecological destruction but also, in the event of war, to the requirements of effectively achieving political objectives at an acceptable cost to one's own country, one's allies, and civilization itself. An unqualified warwinning, country-destroying strategy was unconscionable even when the United States held a virtual monopoly of long-range nuclear striking power. It is more obviously intolerable now that this monopoly has been lost, as the current situation not only magnifies the destructiveness of nuclear war but also undermines the credibility of relying on it to deter and defeat aggression. If an indiscriminate, all-out warwinning strategy were a reliably effective deterrent, it would still be morally unacceptable on grounds of intention. But the fact of the matter is that now it cannot safely be regarded as a reliable deterrent against anything except an indiscriminate nuclear attack when any first-use of nuclear weapons, let alone early and unlimited use, has acquired such an onus within the Western security system—indeed, when even the slightest risk of the failure of a war-winning deterrent incurs the unacceptable moral burden of a commitment to carry out an irrational and self-defeating act.

The finite-deterrence school of rejection, unlike the war-winners, may be credited (generally) with humanitarian sensitivity; but by placing all bets on the infallibility of deterrence, it ignores the perhaps infinitesimal but still terribly significant possibility that the bet might have to be paid off. If the proponents of finite deterrence really intend to carry it out, they are guilty of a morally dubious intention, which even the value of avenging a direct nuclear attack on the United States can scarcely justify, especially if there is the slightest chance of a politically more effective and materially and humanly less damaging response. If the proponents of finite deterrence, (speaking vicariously for the U.S. government) do not really intend to carry out the threat or, despite their intentions, would not actually carry it out if deterrence failed, their dissemblance or deficiency of will incurs an unacceptable risk of encouraging the aggression they seek to deter. And even if the deterrent threat is never challenged, the political and moral strain of sustaining a policy of finite, absolute nuclear deterrence in the United States and Europe would, at the least, leave the Western countries vulnerable to Soviet intimidation and deprive them of that sense of rough military parity without which most of security-related diplomacy—especially arms negotiation—would be impotent.

The only plausible rejectionist retort to these charges is that, in reality, there is no feasible alternative to a strategy of warwinning or finite deterrence, given that once nuclear weapons are used, it is impossible to limit civil damage significantly anyway. But we cannot know that this is true, and there are many developments in strategic doctrine (such as those toward flexible and controlled responses on both sides) and in military technology and plans (especially more accurate conventional as well as nuclear counterforce weapons, which are less prone to collateral damage, and improved C^3I) that make it less likely to be true now and in the future than it may have been through the 1960s.

In any case, considering the certainty that a rejectionist strategy would lead to virtually unlimited civil destruction, the morally relevant question to ask is not, simply, whether it is possible to impose politically significant and humanly tolerable limits on nuclear exchanges but whether it is so certainly impossible that we can responsibly reject the most scrupulous effort to hold open the options of limitation and political control. From this perspective there can be no justification for acting as though such an effort is bound to fail. The claim made by advocates of finite deterrence—that maintaining limited counterforce nuclear options leads to costly and redundant nuclear capabilities—is no argument for an exclusively city-busting strategy, even if one assumes (incorrectly) that the Soviets would play this game.

ABOLITION APPRAISED

The abolitionist approach is morally preferable to the rejectionist approach in that it at least begins by recognizing the moral and practical enormity of the nuclear dilemma. However, the political and material means of achieving abolition do not exist in the real world; and if they did exist, the consequences of abolishing nuclear weapons among adversaries in an anarchy of international relations would be worse than the adverse effects of the system of nuclear deterrence with which we are familiar. Logically, the strongest case for abolition—assuming for the sake of argument that it were attainable—is based on the proposition that the use of nuclear weapons is absolutely evil because the cost would necessarily be an unmitigated catastrophe, disproportionate to the value of any end sought. Of course, if a government really believed this and was determined to act on its belief (a prospect that is hardly imaginable), it should be prepared to renounce nuclear weapons and nuclear deterrence unilaterally and take the consequences.

Then it would at least avoid the slightest risk of being responsible for the use of nuclear weapons, while depriving the adversary of any excuse to use its nuclear weapons. Professed abolitionists, however (except, perhaps, for a tiny group of genuine pacifists), seldom face up to the full logic of their position. Or if they do, it is because they assume that the consequences of unilateral nuclear disarmament would be benign. They may assume that the Soviet Union would constitute no threat once it was relieved of the threat to itself, that force would cease to be an instrument of policy and military equilibrium would no longer be a condition of peace, that world government would solve the nuclear dilemma by wielding a monopoly of force under law, that an ethic of common security and mutual restraint would replace the ethic of competitive insecurity, or that a nonnuclear balance of force would be an effective substitute for nuclear deterrence.

All but the last assumption is so clearly out of touch with reality as to need no discussion here. I have already noted the feasibility and desirability of substituting a nonnuclear, defense-dominant structure of mutual deterrence for a conventional-plus-nuclear balance (see Chapter 5), and I reached a negative conclusion on both counts. It is worth repeating that the vision of mutual deterrence based on nearly perfect conventional shields does not, strictly speaking, eliminate the military basis of the nuclear dilemma, given that (as Jonathan Schell has realized) the threat of nuclear rearmament would remain a factor in deterrence, the arms race, and war. Therefore, on the basis of an elementary understanding of international politics and the role of force, abolitionists cannot escape responsibility for calculating the effect of a structure of deterrence dependent on nuclear rearmament on the stability of a military balance between armed adversaries. The effect seems quite unlikely to be benign.

MITIGATION APPRAISED

For these reasons I believe that the only realistic and ethical approach to coping with the nuclear dilemma is mitigation.

Among armed adversaries with access to nuclear weapons, the state must act on the premise that the nuclear dilemma cannot be completely overcome but only mitigated in various ways and different degrees. As I suggested at the beginning of this book, there are three principal ways of mitigating this dilemma: Make deterrence effective, reduce its dependence on nuclear weapons, and limit the use of nuclear weapons under effective political control if deterrence fails. In some circumstances these three objectives would coincide; in others they would conflict. One can best approach the art of striking the optimal balance among them by appraising them in the context of the maximalist/minimalist spectrum of mitigation as it pertains to the central issues of coping with the nuclear dilemma. The following sections examine these objectives by following this approach.

The Credibility of Deterrence

The maximalists seek to expand the margin of safety (or reduce the risk of error) in deterrence by basing the credibility of deterrence less on the uncertainties of will and resolve—and the intangibles of mutual mind reading—and more on the physical capability to carry out the deterrent threat effectively at a tolerable cost. For this reason they prefer to rely on denial capabilities rather than punitive measures. They emphasize the necessity of reducing dependence on nuclear retaliation and nuclear first-use (especially early first-use) and the value of bringing all kinds of force, including nuclear force, under limitation and political control. Given all the military and political factors that have been eroding the credibility of nuclear deterrence, and the disastrous consequences if deterrence should fail, this is a prudent approach, which is especially compelling when it comes to deterring conventional attacks with threatened nuclear responses.

But the minimalists warn that this approach, if carried too far, will weaken deterrence by indicating a lack of will to incur the unavoidable risk of exorbitant costs. Logically, it is a strange point for minimalists to make, given their relative confidence that existential deterrence, based on the inherent destructive potential of nuclear armaments, will keep the peace despite great disparities of fighting strength. But in matters of deterrence, perfect logic is not necessarily the mark of common sense. Maximalist reasoning, too, suffers from the necessity of coping with conflicting objectives. Thus, if the strategic balance is as delicate—as dependent on the relative military capability of the adversary to achieve a marginal advantage by striking first—as the maximalists claim, one can argue that it is dangerous to encourage the Soviets to think that the prospect of a nuclear response to extreme provocation depends primarily on relative warfighting capabilities, unless we can be sure that we enjoy a decisive warfighting disadvantage and that the Soviets know it. The practical importance of this minimalist argument depends not only on what the balance of warfighting capabilities is, but also on what the Soviets think it is and what risks they may be willing to incur in order to exploit a warfighting advantage. If the United States and its allies cannot, in fact, develop conventional and nuclear responses that are such effective instruments of denial and so readily subject to limitation as to be profitable to carry out, it is more prudent to follow the minimalists' advice to base deterrence on a large element of uncertainty and sheer national resolve, unimpeded by refined calculations of unpredictable consequences. Regrettably, this condition is the reality. Yet the reality can be improved.

In extended deterrence, given the obvious geographical, political, and economic impediments to a completely effective nonnuclear response to Soviet nonnuclear aggression, minimum prudence requires that the nuclear threshold be raised to at least a credible capacity to avoid having to consider nuclear escalation within the first two weeks of a major clash of conventional arms. The collective political will should be up to this task; however, it is an unanswerable question as to whether improving conventional resistance much further, if feasible, would enhance or weaken extended deterrence. But as a demonstration of collective will, any strengthening of NATO's conventional forces should have an inhibiting effect on the Soviet mind. By the same token, however, if an American effort to push its allies into greater conventional denial efforts is not acceptable to the allies, this situation will send a deterrence-weakening signal to the Soviets. In other words, the minimalists are correct, up to a point, in arguing that the most impressive deterrent is allied cohesion in behalf of an assured response to aggression; so it makes sense to trade off some potential denial capability for collective strategic consensus—as, indeed, MC 14/3 exemplifies. If this trade-off necessitates a declaratory determination to meet aggression with a response that would be ineffectual and counterproductive—indeed, politically impossible—to carry out, it is better, although not more moral, to affirm the White Lie than to confess the Dark Truth and still have to live with the lie.

Direct deterrence—that is, deterring a Soviet first strike against the United States—does not raise the question of credibility except in the most theoretical way; there can be no doubt in the Soviet mind that the United States would retaliate, but there must be a great deal of doubt that the resulting nuclear exchanges could be significantly and advantageously limited. It would be irrational to imagine that the Soviet Union, even in a crisis far more intense than Berlin or Cuba, would see an advantage in striking first (even if its military intelligence indicated a grave risk of being struck first) because of some mathematical calculation that it could disarm more than 90 percent of U.S. ICBMs with one-third of its strategic strike force and leave the United States with only a countervalue retaliatory capability—to so imagine is to assume that Soviet leaders would uncharacteristically act like the wildest gamblers. If the Soviets know that the United States has more than a finite minimal capacity to inflict unacceptable damage (and this is certainly the case), it is even more improbable that they would strike first because of some calculation of relative advantage in exchange ratios and the like. Surely, the minimalists are correct in their contention that within a great disparity of quantitative nuclear inferiority—whether in first- or second-strike capabilities—the political psychology of existential deterrence ensures against a Soviet first strike. Nevertheless, the maximalists' great concern about windows of vulnerability and other metaphysical expressions of warfighting inferiority makes political-psychological sense, up to a point that the minimalists often fail to appreciate. The minimalists

recognize that disparities of national will impinge upon that
will in conflicts well below the threshold of war. They recognize
that passive acceptance of an adverse trend in the military
balance, over time, may have a debilitating effect on a whole
range of state-to-state relations, even if it does not tempt
military aggression. In intense crises a numerically impressive
Soviet first-strike advantage, coupled with a highly vulnerable
U.S. land-based retaliatory force, might, as the maximalists
claim, provide the Soviets with a dangerous bargaining and
intimidating lever, depending on the balance of interests and
the balance of conventional forces at the point of crisis. This
kind of psychopolitical danger is only loosely related to deterrence; but if it is consistently neglected, it may erode
deterrence itself.

This point argues in favor of not conceding too large a
margin of effective counterforce warfighting capability to the
Soviets, even though both sides know that, however precise
the strikes against military targets might be, the results would
probably be tantamount to national suicide long before a
fraction of the total warheads had found their target. The
point simply reflects the realities of great-power competition
in the cloudy but significant realm of power politics short of
war. To argue its imperatives under the name of either prewar
or intrawar deterrence stretches the meaning of deterrence;
but the minimalists, who emphasize the importance of will and
resolve in deterrence, should be the first to appreciate the
danger that subjective impressions of relative power, if left
unattended, may objectively affect the calculations of states
about the actual use of force.

Of course, any sound strategic insight becomes nonsense if
driven to extremes. Therefore, it is important to understand
that in matters of deterrence-credibility the difference between
sense and nonsense depends far more on the total political
context within which the competition for military strength
takes place than on the precise margins of technical superiority
or inferiority. This is particularly true with respect to extended
deterrence, where estimates of the credibility of deterrence in
the Soviet mind must be continually infused with and balanced
by considerations of reassurance to allies.

The Limitations of Nuclear Force

The most difficult strategic issues, morally and ethically, pertain not so much to the credibility of deterrence as to the use of force if deterrence should fail; and the most difficult issues of use arise with respect to nuclear weapons. Only rejectionists, pure abolitionists, and absolute pacifists can avoid, in their own consciences, the moral and practical problems that arise from the fact that the threat or commitment to use nuclear weapons as a deterrent entails a willingness to carry out the threat and that, therefore, extreme risks and costs of nuclear use are intrinsic to nuclear deterrence. On grounds of morality, as much as expediency, the serious question is not how to avoid the nuclear dilemma but how to mitigate it. But those who believe that they can ignore or escape this reality through warfighting superiority, infallible deterrence, the elimination of nuclear weapons, or complete military abstention are morally naive or ethically irresponsible. How one copes with the issue of nuclear use depends on how one views the doctrine of just war and its applicability and application to nuclear war.[69]

If the principles of just war—just cause, exhaustion of peaceful alternatives, competent authority, effective means, proportionality, and minimum civil damage—apply at all to nuclear use, the necessary condition is that the use of nuclear weapons not be beyond political control and physical limitation. Otherwise, considering the extremities of undiscriminating nuclear war, it is indeed difficult (although not intellectually impossible or philosophically absurd) to disagree with the premise of finite deterrence and abolitionism that no *casus belli* can be worth the catastrophic cost of nuclear war. If, on the other hand, truly significant control and limitation of nuclear exchanges appear to be feasible (or, at least, not clearly and absolutely infeasible), then all the principles of just war are applicable; and it is the moral duty of states to translate them into military plans and operations. Significant limitation and control must be measured, above all, by the capacity of the victim of aggression to end the war without inflicting a degree of civil damage upon itself, its allies, the enemy, and others that would be so excessive as to nullify the values at stake.

A prudent consideration of the application of just-war doctrine to nuclear use must acknowledge the great uncertainty—indeed, improbability—of any such significant limitation. It follows that the case for militarily flexible and politically controlled use of nuclear weapons should be based on choosing the lesser evil in the most extreme case. It must be based on the goal of gaining some insurance against the irrational use of force if deterrence fails rather than on enhancing the credibility of, or increasing the reliance upon, nuclear deterrence. Therefore, the maximalists' strongest case for flexible and controlled strategic nuclear options (and the one emphasized by the maximalists themselves) is not the enhancement of deterrence but the rationalization of the overt use of nuclear weapons, in recognition of the fact that the prospect of overt use is inherent in nuclear deterrence.

The objection of some minimalists that such a strategy will tempt the United States to take unreasonable risks of nuclear war simply does not correspond to the psychological reality of the immense inhibitions that the United States and its allies operate under in facing the slightest risk of nuclear war. No theoretical scenario of limited nuclear exchanges can obviate either the immense uncertainties about their working in reality or the certainty of senseless catastrophe if they fail to work.

The best arguments against a determined effort to develop limited nuclear options are that (1) there is a negligible risk that the nuclear deterrent will actually have to be carried out and that (2) the effort to develop the option is bound to be both inordinately expensive because of its stimulus to the counterforce arms race and, most important, (3) completely futile.

The first argument—the argument of infallible deterrence—reflects the same kind of imprudence that underlies the strategy of finite deterrence. The second argument—concerning the stimilation of a costly counterforce race—is true only on the assumption that both sides would confine their strategic objective to targeting a limited number of cities. In reality, this assumption is not confirmed by the observable dynamics of the postwar arms competition. Even if the United States were to pursue a strategy of finite deterrence, it is very doubtful that the Soviets would reciprocate. It is also doubtful that, given the magnitude of present counterforce capabilities, U.S. targeting plans will affect the intensity of the strategic arms competition one way or the other. With respect to the third argument—that significantly limited nuclear exchanges are impossible—my contention is that the burden of proof should lie with those who categorically insist that there is no possibility of significantly limiting nuclear exchanges, not on those who believe that the only responsible course is to make every reasonable effort to hold open the possibility. No evidence nor inference from experience warrants excluding such efforts on the grounds that they are inevitably futile. The alternative position—either planning to wage undiscriminating nuclear war or not planning to fight a nuclear war at all—is morally unconscionable.

Nevertheless, if one concedes, as I do, that there is a very great risk that the best efforts to limit and control nuclear war will fail, one must also conclude that any actual use of nuclear weapons—whether against conventional or nuclear aggression—entails a very great risk of waging war unjustly. Then the ethical question becomes whether the state is morally obliged to refrain from nuclear use despite its commitment to the contrary and despite the adverse consequences of abstaining, or whether reason of state should prevail over an effort to avoid a grave moral risk. Considering the practical difficulty of reconciling a credible deterrent commitment to use nuclear weapons with a commitment to refrain from using them when the occasion arises, there is much to be said for leaving the question of nuclear use or abstention open rather than deciding to abstain in advance.

For the protection of Western Europe, as distinguished from the prevention of direct attacks against the United States, limited nuclear options, under present political, economic, and technological conditions, are an indispensable deterrent as well as a necessary hedge against the failure of deterrence. These are preeminent values. But this is not to say that the prospect of significantly limiting the use of nuclear weapons, tactical or strategic, demonstrative or otherwise, can be contemplated with confidence or that it should make the use of nuclear weapons anything but a desperate last resort. There is certainly good cautionary sense in the minimalists' warning that, especially in the densely packed urban areas of geographically confined Western Europe, the risk is immense that collateral damage and escalation would soon push the most finely restricted and cleverly bargained use of nuclear weapons toward catastrophe.

The more one considers the technical difficulties (e.g., maintaining effective C^3I) and political problems (e.g., the differential vulnerability of Western Europe) of conducting a significantly limited nuclear war, the more one is driven to the conclusion that only early war termination can give nuclear limitation any rational political meaning. Experts inside and outside the government—always sensitive to the onus of ending a momentously costly war by compromising with the enemy—have given too little attention to the operational military and political implications of early war termination.[70] Of course, there is no guarantee that a great deal of attention would enable us to mitigate substantially the costs and risks of nuclear use. A nuclear war is likely to be started deliberately for exceedingly high political stakes—not merely because of a political miscalculation. Yet the prospect of ending such a war early presupposes a willingness of one side or both to relinquish its political objective before fully subjecting it to the test of force. On the other hand, the special trauma of any nuclear exchange is more likely to induce an attitude of urgent reconsideration and withdrawal than one of militant escalation. If the implementation of this attitude was not left to improvisation but, instead, was prepared in advance, early termination of even a nuclear exchange might be possible.

The immense difficulty of formulating, let alone putting into practice, a strategy of limited nuclear war in which policymakers can have any confidence indicates that deciding upon the applicability of just-war principles to nuclear use only confronts us with the much more formidable problem of how to apply these principles. This problem of application is one aspect of the general problem of applying the principle of proportionality, which is crucial to the whole doctrine of *jus in bello.* The very concept of proportionality is so ambiguous and elastic as to be of questionable significance. Does it mean that the civilian damage caused by military defense of a just cause should not be disproportionate to the value of the cause? If so, how does one equate and measure against each other the disparate elements of this benefit-cost calculus? Perhaps the concept can be simplified so that it becomes roughly equivalent to the economy of force—that is, to the principle that no greater force should be used than is necessary to achieve the political objective in question. But unless the nature and degree of force are related to their moral cost and to the extent of civilian damage in particular, the economy-of-force principle is so open-ended as to provide the most conscientious war-fighters with only the loosest kind of guidance about practical restraints on the use of force.

Especially when one considers its application to nuclear weapons, the principle of proportionality needs to be supplemented by other principles more subject to operational translation. Foremost among these is the principle of discrimination, which prohibits direct and intentional damage to noncombatants (especially in population centers) and militarily avoidable collateral civil damage from attacks on military targets. Yet acceptance of this principle leaves open a number of practical strategic issues. Surely, proper discrimination requires the reciprocal avoidance of cities, but what about other counter-value targets, such as military-industrial facilities and command centers? What if civilian targets are physically inseparable from legitimate military targets, as is not uncommon in the Soviet Union or Western Europe? What if the Soviets strike at U.S. population centers or those of the European allies? How does one manage a trade-off between maximizing military advantage and minimizing collateral damage? If, under some imaginable conditions, limited countervalue retaliatory attacks seem more likely to produce early and satisfactory war termination than limited counterforce retaliation attacks, should we still prefer the latter on moral grounds?

The great difficulty of answering these questions counsels against basing deterrence strategies on anything but the most tentative and conditional assumption that nuclear weapons can serve the principles of Clausewitz or just war if deterrence fails. But it does not in the slightest degree argue against the maximalists' insistence that the only morally responsible approach is to devote an intensive effort to validate this assumption. At the same time, it surely reinforces the urgency of the mitigators' axiom that a doctrine of just deterrence demands the minimum practicable reliance upon nuclear weapons that is consistent with deterrence of the Soviet Union and reassurance to the United States' allies.

Implications for the Arms Race

The major complaint of many minimalists about the maximalist approach to mitigating the nuclear dilemma—and one that was at the core of the ABM debate—is that a damage-limiting strategy, whether implemented by counterforce strikes or active defense measures or both, intensifies the arms race and is therefore both expensive and provocative. The corollary of this complaint is the proposition that to refrain conspicuously from the effort to limit damage, so as to reinforce the unavoidability of mutual assured destruction, fosters moderation of the arms race and the stability of deterrence, especially if parity of MAD capabilities is codified in an arms agreement.

As maximalist analysts have argued, the minimalists' complaint is based on an erroneously simplistic understanding of the observable dynamics of the arms competition.[71] The structure and intensity of East-West arms competition spring from several different sources, some of which bear no direct relation to the "action-reaction" phenomenon. Neither the steadiness of Soviet arms investments and programs nor the ups and downs of U.S. arms investments and programs can be explained by the vulnerability of national populations to retaliatory destruction or by the efforts to limit this vulnerability. Nor is there any evidence that parity of MAD capabilities, even when codified in an arms agreement, dampens the arms competition. The history of SALT comes closer to supporting the opposite conclusion.

Furthermore, whatever the intensity of the arms competition may be, its effect on East-West political relations depends on many factors in addition to the arms competition, as demonstrated both by the period of détente and by its breakdown in the 1970s (when U.S. defense expenditures were declining and strategic deployments were languishing). Insofar as the intensity of the arms competition depends on the structure of forces, the maximalists' operating assumption is that stability or instability is what counts and that instability is primarily a function of the fear of either side that the other has a usable first-strike capability. This assumption, too, oversimplifies a complex phenomenon, but it at least sets a fairly tangible and attainable standard for measuring military equilibrium. There is a presumption in favor of a perceived equilibrium fostering safer and more moderate relations between armed adversaries. But the relationship of equilibrium or disequilibrium to the intensity of the arms race and to the quality of East-West relations in general is too complex to yield to any correlation based on the single factor of U.S. counterforce programs and capabilities.

All these arguments aside, the obvious point that the minimalist critique ignores or instinctively dismisses is that, whatever the impact of a counterforce damage-limiting or any other kind of deterrence strategy may be on the arms race, a judgment about its expediency and morality should be based on whether the cost of this impact is worth paying relative to the value of the end the strategy seeks to attain. Only a skewed sense of priorities leads automatically to the assumption that the material cost or political provocation of an intensified arms competition must be disproportionate to the value of the deterrence objective. Of course, if the means of deterrence do not achieve the intended results, no effort to support the means would be worthwhile, whatever the impact on the arms race. But that is a different issue.

The Morality of Hostages

What does this all mean for the validity of the competing moral claims of maximalists and minimalists with respect to

holding national populations hostage to nuclear obliteration?[72]
At the center of the maximalists' moral claim is the assertion
that it is unethical that deterrence should be based, ultimately,
on East and West holding each other's national populations
hostage to assured destruction. Therefore, to moderate the
moral cost of deterrence, they conclude, everything possible
should be done to reduce and (supporters of SDI would say)
eventually eliminate the dependence of both sides on nuclear
retaliation, and also to limit the damage from retaliation in
case deterrence fails. In defending existential MAD, the minimalists do not claim that holding nations hostage under the
threat of mutual suicide is morally edifying but only that the
predicament is unavoidable and that maximalist efforts to
remedy the predicament encourage the dangerous illusion that
nuclear weapons can be used without suicidal results. A policy
based on this concept of utility would be more immoral in its
consequences (or, in the terms of this book, more costly in
moral values) than are efforts to make MAD as stable and
safe as possible.

It follows from the preceding discussion of contrasting strategies of deterrence that the maximalist position has the stronger
moral case, but only providing that the hedges against mutual
suicide are regarded as a kind of desperate insurance against
catastrophe, not as an enhancement of deterrence or an incentive to take greater risks of a nuclear encounter—in short,
as anything more than a fragile and uncertain mitigation of
the terrible probability that nuclear war would be catastrophic.
With these qualifications, the maximalist position draws the
better balance between the efficacy of deterrence, reduced
dependence on nuclear deterrence, and limited use of nuclear
weapons if deterrence fails. It comes closer to relating consequences to ends in terms of the effectiveness and proportionality of the means. It does not, however, nullify the minimalists' basic position that, for the foreseeable future, extended
nuclear deterrence must depend on the West's threat of nuclear
escalation, that direct deterrence must depend on the threat
of nuclear retaliation, and that the ultimate deterrent in both
cases must unavoidably be the great likelihood that any nuclear
response to aggression will lead to unacceptable civil damage.

The minimalists err, not when they affirm this existential basis of mutual deterrence, but when they deprecate efforts to mitigate its consequences.

Nuclear First-Use

The most contentious issue at stake in competing maximalist and minimalist moral claims is nuclear first-use in support of extended deterrence. As I noted in my examination of the American controversy on this issue, maximalists and minimalists line up on both sides of the debate; but the maximalist supporters of a no-nuclear first-use posture, unlike the minimalist supporters, do not advocate a declaratory renunciation. The philosophical, emotional, and material grounds for these contrasting positions are fairly clear. Much less clear are the grounds upon which all critics of nuclear first-use, and most supporters, assume that nuclear first-use bears a distinctly greater moral onus than nuclear second-use. Thus, it is not clear why the American Catholic bishops condemn the former absolutely but the latter only conditionally.

The reason for this distinction seems so obvious that its proponents never feel the need to explain it, but its obviousness may be more instinctive than reasoned. Perhaps it springs from a misapplication of the standards of personal morality to interstate ethics, in that it unquestioningly sanctions an act of vengeance that may be valid for an aggrieved individual but is extremely hard to justify among states—especially in the case of direct nuclear exchanges between the superpowers. What is the sense or morality of inflicting catastrophic retaliatory damage at the cost of incurring reciprocal damage? Individuals may legitimately ignore a reasoned calculation of the consequences of an act of vengeance if it corresponds to a socially sanctioned code of ethics, but states have a moral obligation to consider the relationship of means to ends when the consequences of vengeance exceed any rational bounds.

Is the moral distinction between first-use and second-use based on a difference of value regarding the end for which nuclear weapons would be used? In the global scheme of U.S. interests, is not the security of Western Europe integrally entangled with, if not identical to, the security of the United States? If the distinction is based on the rational relationship of means and consequences to the end, it is difficult to see why nuclear retaliation against the USSR in response to a Soviet nuclear attack on the United States is more moral than nuclear escalation in response to a Soviet-led conventional attack against Western Europe. Indeed, the latter response may be somewhat more susceptible to a politically significant limitation of the conflict and to the opportunity to stop short of the threshold of nuclear winter. It would seem to lend itself to the decision to take military steps of an obviously counterforce nature more slowly up the escalation ladder, so as to maximize opportunities for early war termination—particularly in light of the greater possibility that the initial military encounter would almost surely have been precipitated by a more limited political conflict with a greater possibility of miscalculation. From this standpoint, extended deterrence, in the event that it was carried out, seems less likely than direct deterrence to be tantamount to an act of suicidal vengeance. At the same time, if the deterrent works, it is far less dependent on the intended threat of nuclear retaliation.

Therefore, if the special opposition to nuclear first-use is based simply on the view that the unavoidably inordinate destruction of East-West nuclear exchanges can have no rational or moral purpose, as the Catholic bishops argue, it makes no sense; for the same view should lead to at least equal and, arguably, greater condemnation of a nuclear response to a nuclear attack. If this view is based on the proposition that commitment to nuclear first-use betrays a morally irresponsible preference for running the risk of nuclear war instead of incurring the cost of nonnuclear defense, as some maximalists argue, this makes a great deal of sense; but the onus must fall on Western society, not on those who reluctantly adapt deterrence strategy to the political realities of budgetary and manpower constraints while trying to relieve these constraints. Actually, in the absence of argumentation, one suspects that the sharp moral distinction between nuclear first- and second-use springs from visceral sentiment rather than the kind of rigorous moral reasoning that should weigh the optimal balance among ends, means, and consequences. This kind of sentiment undermines the credibility of extended deterrence without supporting the means of mitigating the consequences. Obviously, the now-commonplace endorsement by those most moralistically opposed to nuclear first-use (including theologians and European left-wing socialists) of stronger conventional capabilities to compensate for the abolition of a nuclear response to conventional aggression is a rhetorical gesture better calculated to justify strategic self-abnegation than to mobilize material support for a military build-up.

Restructuring Deterrence

The task of mitigating the nuclear dilemma by reducing dependence on nuclear weapons and enhancing the efficacy of limited and controlled military responses while strengthening deterrence is not only exceedingly important on the grounds of both morality and expediency; it is also feasible. But given the formidable constraints in Western society against the material sacrifices required, the extent of mitigation must be very limited. It remains to be seen whether a more substantial mitigation of the nuclear dilemma (although it would fall far short of abolition) can be achieved by developing defensive weapons against offensive nuclear weapons, by substituting nonnuclear weapons for some functions now performed by nuclear weapons, and by combining the conventionalization of weaponry with agreed-upon nuclear arms reductions and limitations.

For the purpose of enhancing extended deterrence with reduced dependence on nuclear weapons, much of the conventional technology (such as precision-guided munitions and C^{3}I) has already been developed, although its cost-effectiveness and affordability and its comparative value with respect to less exotic conventional defense measures are in question and there is no firm consensus on its tactical implications. In the next decade or two, conventional air defense against nuclear and conventional warheads will almost certainly be improved by the development of ATBMs that are considerably more effective than the existing Soviet first-generation SA-X-12. Optimistic assumptions suggest that this diversified technology, in conjunction with other improvements in air defense, may eventually raise the nuclear threshold substantially. In this case the question will arise as to whether the effects on the credibility of deterrence and the rational utility of carrying it out are likely to be, on balance, favorable or unfavorable. According to the bias of this book, the answer lies in the direction of the maximalists' position, qualified by the minimalists' sensitivity to the political requirements of allied cohesion.

With respect to direct deterrence, the hope for more substantial mitigation of the nuclear dilemma probably lies less in further technical improvements in the limitation and control of nuclear weapons than in the prospect of a more defense-reliant structure of deterrence, constructed on the basis of nonnuclear BMD and supplemented by the development of nonnuclear offensive weapons. As previously noted, the infeasibility and, I would contend, undesirability of nearly perfect defensive systems for East and West does not argue against the possibility and value of a 70 percent (or less) effective protection of military sites, with a significant civilian damage-limiting bonus (especially in Western Europe). In the context of an arms agreement providing for deep reductions of strategic nuclear warheads, which the deployment of strategic-defense weapons should help to achieve and stabilize, such a defense-reliant structure might foster the limitation and control of strategic exchanges and early war termination, diminish the likelihood of nuclear winter, and, at the same time, be no less effective a deterrent than the present structure.

In the proposed defense-reliant structure, counterforce functions would largely be performed by nonnuclear weapons, but a minimal stockpile of strategic nuclear weapons would remain. It can be argued—but by no means irrefutably—that these remaining strategic nuclear weapons would be targeted against cities, as these would be the only profitable targets to strike, given the protection of military sites. If so, there would also be an argument for a strategy of limited nuclear countervalue retaliation. This development would be an ironic consequence of measures designed to reduce reliance on nuclear retaliation; but, even so, these circumstances would be a material and ethical improvement over the existing situation, in which the deliberate avoidance of cities, in the absence of early war termination, offers such faint hope of avoiding the escalation of nuclear exchanges to catastrophic dimensions.

This vision of a Partially Defended World is, to put it moderately, fraught with unknown variables and predictable problems. Not the least of the problems is that of managing an orderly transition. To offset mutual fears that the enhancement of defensive capabilities would also enhance first-strike capabilities, the altered mix of defense to offense ought to be effected through phased arms agreements limiting offensive as well as defensive weapons.

The difficulty of achieving a stable transition is exaggerated by those who charge that any increase of defensive capabilities will be destabilizing. This charge concentrates on the possibility that enhanced defense might encourage a first strike by limiting the adversary's capacity to inflict retaliatory damage, but it does not weigh this possibility against the increased uncertainty that a first strike could effectively disarm the retaliatory force. From what we know about the relative constraints against a first- and second-strike, it seems reasonable to suppose that enhanced antimissile defenses would exert greater constraint on the country striking first than on the country retaliating.

The problem of a stable transition to a more defense-reliant structure of deterrence is not primarily that the changing offense-defense ratio would be destabilizing in the sense that it would seriously increase the likelihood of a nuclear first-strike. Given the diversity of the weapons, the protracted period of time in which they would be introduced, the uncertainty about how they would operate in wartime, and the reluctance of either side to deploy weapons that were incapable of surviving attacks on them, there is no reason to think that the introduction of this vast array of technology would be more destabilizing than ICBMs, MIRVs, cruise missiles, or other new weapons and weapons improvements have been in the past—especially if one assumes that both sides have an interest in an orderly transition. The problem lies in the fundamental political difficulty that adversaries have in reaching agreement on how to measure, equate, and restrict opposing forces with the precision and duration required by a formal treaty in order to improve their relative military positions (such improvement always being the first objective of both sides). In order to get mutual defense-reliant structures, both sides would have to reach an agreement on how to reduce offensive systems and keep them suppressed while introducing defensive systems under ceilings. But the hardest thing for armed adversaries to agree on in a treaty that specifies mutual restrictions in legally binding and verifiable detail is an altered balance of military power. Freezing the existing balance is difficult enough; codifying an altered balance, based on offensive reductions and defensive increases, is several times more difficult. And one must be particularly skeptical that the Soviets have an interest in codifying any American concept of a stable military balance.

We must face the possibility (indeed, the probability) that solving this problem of cooperative transition—which would require, among other things, the orderly, phased revision of the ABM Treaty—is not compatible with the minimal extent of converging interests and mutual trust that Washington and Moscow can muster. It is far more likely that the treaty will gradually erode through circumvention and neglect as its obsolescence becomes increasingly obvious. The actual dynamics of arms races provide no reason to assume that the result of this rechanneling of arms competition would lead to the kind of perilous, wildly spiraling arms race that common wisdom has regarded as the inevitable consequence of the failure of disarmament or arms control ever since the beginning of the nuclear age. But neither would it produce the kind of defense-reliant balance envisioned in the moderate version of SDI's goal. Rather, it would produce a much more complex mix of offensive and defensive weapons in which nuclear retaliation would still be the core of deterrence, while the relationship of offense to defense would resume its traditional dynamics, temporarily aborted by the ABM Treaty. If arms agreements can be reached under these conditions (and constant efforts will certainly be made to reach them), either they will be more limited agreements to restrict weapons that make the least difference to the overall East-West military balance, or they will be comprehensive agreements that essentially codify existing balances that have reached a state of equilibrium between periods of competition relatively unconstrained by agreements.

CONCLUDING REMARKS

A world of rapidly proliferating offensive and defensive weapons in space, land, and sea might be no less stable or even substantially more stable, as objectively appraised, than the world of the 1970s or 1980s. The history of arms races thus far provides no basis for assured prediction. Subjectively and politically, however, this world would be full of organized anxieties and alarms on the part of those who are primarily concerned about military security as well as those primarily concerned about the perils of war. The abolitionists would dominate the latter group, but the controversies that directly affect the decisions of governments would resound across the full maximalist/minimalist spectrum of mitigation.

To a degree, however, this will be true in any case, regardless of the extent to which arms agreements enter into the process of arms competition. Although arms agreements may usefully constrain or rechannel some segments of the competition, they cannot stop technological innovation or even slow down the totality of weapons research, development, testing, and production. Much less can they eliminate or even moderate the political sources of rivalry that underlie the competition for military security and advantage. But to come to terms with the limits of arms control is simply to recognize that as long as there are armed adversaries with access to advanced technology, the nuclear dilemma will be with us. To pretend that the goal of abolishing this dilemma can be even approximated is to surrender the guidance of reason and experience to the ephemeral gratification of sentiments nurtured by sheer hope or public deception.

Notes

1. The dictionary definition of *dilemma*, contrary to the meta-phorical predicament of being caught on the horns of a dilemma, does not preclude an optimal choice that would gain some of the advantages of one course of action while mitigating the disadvantages of an associated course of action. It only precludes a completely satisfactory solution of the problem of choice. This study makes no precise distinction between the "moral" and "ethical" aspects of strategic choices. Generally, morality refers to the right-principled or ideal quality of a course of action taken by a person or a government; ethics refers to the code or system of moral principles applied to such a course of action.

2. With his rather mischievous imagination, Kahn invented the notion of the Doomsday Machine in the late 1950s to show the absurdity of the prevailing strategy of responding to aggression with an all-out nuclear blow when the Soviets could retaliate in kind. In theory, it consisted of a huge world-wide array of H-bombs, wired to destroy all human life and automatically set to detonate upon a computer-sensed Soviet aggression. See Herman Kahn, *On Thermonuclear War* (Princeton, N.J.: Princeton University Press, 1960), pp. 144–160.

3. David Allen Rosenberg, "A Smoking Radiating Ruin at the End of Two Hours: Documents on American Plans for Nuclear War with the Soviet Union, 1954–1955," *International Security*, vol. 6 (Winter 1981/1982), 3–38; David Allen Rosenberg, "The Origins of Overkill: Nuclear Weapons and American Strategy, 1945–1960," *International Security*, vol. 7 (Spring 1983), 11–16.

4. Thus, in a public address in November 1954, Dulles explained that the strategy termed "massive retaliation" had never meant that "any local war would automatically be turned into a general war with atomic bombs being dropped all over the map." "The important

thing," he said, was that "we and our allies should have the means and the will to assure that a potential aggressor would lose from his aggression more than he could win." See his speech to the National 4-H Clubs Congress in Chicago (November 29, 1954), printed in *Department of State Bulletin*, vol. 31 (December 13, 1954), 892.

5. This interpretation is well documented in John Lewis Gaddis's unpublished manuscript, "The Origins of Self-Deterrence: The United States and the Non-Use of Nuclear Weapons, 1945–1958" (n.d.), in which the record of NSC meetings recounting Eisenhower's and Dulles's arguments against using nuclear weapons is particularly significant.

6. Ibid.

7. See Eisenhower's remarks on the Berlin crisis in a press conference, *New York Times*, March 12, 1959, p. 12; and his remarks at a state dinner in Manila, in ibid., June 16, 1960, p. 14.

8. William W. Kaufmann, in his famous criticism of the strategy of massive retaliation (see *The Requirements of Deterrence*, Memorandum No. 7, Princeton, N.J., Center of International Studies, 1954), conceded this point on the grounds that most Americans regarded Western Europe as an area of vital interests and were therefore willing to use nuclear weapons to defend it. Bernard Brodie agreed in "Unlimited Weapons and Limited War," *Reporter*, November 18, 1954, pp. 16–21.

9. Robert Gilpin, *American Scientists and Nuclear Weapons Policy* (Princeton, N.J.: Princeton University Press, 1962), ch. 2.

10. Nevil Shute, *On the Beach* (New York: Morrow, Williams & Co., 1957).

11. See Robert A. Levine's analysis of the "anti-war systemists" in his elaborate breakdown of attitudes toward nuclear weapons entitled *The Arms Debate* (Cambridge: Harvard University Press, 1963), pp. 282–305. On the U.S. peace movement and the "Professional Left," who supported abolition and finite deterrence, see Adam M. Garfinkle, *The Politics of the Nuclear Freeze* (Philadelphia: Foreign Policy Research Institute, 1984), ch. 1. Paul Boyer traces the ascendance of antinuclear sentiment among elite groups and in popular culture before 1950 in *By The Bomb's Early Light: American Thought and Culture at the Dawn of the Atomic Age* (New York: Pantheon Books, 1985).

12. Adam Garfinkle examines in detail the rise, diffusion, and fall of the freeze movement in *The Politics of the Nuclear Freeze.*

13. The controversies about military strategy and arms control to which I refer under this label are comprehensively examined in Fred Kaplan, *The Wizards of Armageddon* (New York: Simon and Schuster, 1983), and in Gregg Herken, *Counsels of War* (New York: Alfred A. Knopf, 1985). The latter is more comprehensive but less penetrating in its analysis of substantive positions; it is also less reliable on details.

14. The test of the utility of this distinction is whether it helps to explain the intellectual sources of specific controversies over military strategy and programs and arms control, not whether individual advocates can be placed in one group or another. Nevertheless, with considerable room for argument in less than ten cases, I would categorize individuals (in no order of listing) as follows: *Maximalists:* Albert Wohlstetter, William Kaufmann, Paul Nitze, Herman Kahn, Fred Ikle, Andrew Marshall, Harry Rowen, Colin Gray, Fred Hoffmann, Zbigniew Brzezinski, Samuel Huntington, Alain Enthoven, Klaus Knorr, and Edward Teller. *Minimalists:* McGeorge Bundy, Robert McNamara (except in his initial counterforce damage-limitation phase), Morton Halperin, Robert Jervis, Richard Garwin, Paul Warnke, Jeremy Stone, Spurgeon Keeny, George Rathjens, and James King. Less clearly, on the maximalist side of the maximalist/minimalist spectrum but combining elements of both and, therefore, best placed in the center (or center-maximalist) position are Henry Kissinger, James Schlesinger, Harold Brown, Robert Osgood, Richard Betts, Joseph Nye, Robert Komer, Glenn Snyder. The special cases of Bernard Brodie, Donald Brennan, and Thomas Schelling are discussed at the end of this section.

15. McGeorge Bundy, in an article on the American Catholic Bishops' moral critique of nuclear deterrence, argued that the immense destructive power of nuclear weapons, combined with our uncertainty about the exact consequences of using them in a war, constitute irreducible existential properties of nuclear arsenals, which deter their use apart from detailed statements of strategy. See Bundy, "The Bishops and the Bomb," *New York Review of Books*, June 10, 1983. The concept of existential deterrence was not uncommon before Bundy wrote on the subject. Indeed, it was stated by Bernard Brodie in the latter half of the 1940s. Thus, Brodie observed in *The Absolute Weapon* (New York: Harcourt and Brace, 1946), p. 52, that "everything about the atomic bomb is overshadowed by the twin facts that it exists and that its destructive power is fantastically great."

16. Ibid., Brodie, *The Absolute Weapon*, p. 76.

17. Bernard Brodie, "Changing Capabilities and War Objectives," Bernard Brodie Papers, Box 12, UCLA Library, pp. 28–29.

18. Bernard Brodie, *Strategy in the Missile Age* (Princeton, N.J.: Princeton University Press, 1959).

19. Bernard Brodie, *Escalation and the Nuclear Option* (Princeton, N.J.: Princeton University Press, 1966).

20. Donald G. Brennan, ed., *Arms Control, Disarmament, and National Security* (New York: George Brazilier, 1961).

21. Donald G. Brennan, "What Price Conventional Capabilities in Europe?" *The Reporter,* May 23, 1963; Bernard Brodie, "The McNamara Phenomenon," *World Politics,* vol. 17 (July 1965), 672–686.

22. Thomas C. Schelling, "Comment," in Klaus Knorr and Thornton Read, eds., *Limited Strategic War* (New York: Praeger Publishers, 1962), ch. 8.

23. Thomas C. Schelling, *Arms and Influence* (New Haven, Conn.: Yale University Press, 1966), ch. 5 ("The Diplomacy of Ultimate Survival").

24. Schelling, "Surprise Attack and Disarmament," in Klaus Knorr, ed., *NATO and American Security* (Princeton, N.J.: Princeton University Press, 1959), pp. 206–208.

25. Schelling, *The Strategy of Conflict* (Cambridge: Harvard University Press, 1960).

26. Steven L. Rearden, *The Evolution of American Strategic Doctrine: Paul H. Nitze and the Soviet Challenge* (Boulder, Colo.: Westview Press, with The John Hopkins Foreign Policy Institute, 1984). NSC 68 is reprinted in the Appendix.

27. Ibid., pp. 112–113.

28. Ibid., p. 119.

29. The report of the committee (under the title "Deterrence and Survival in the Nuclear Age"), chaired by H. Rowan Gaither, was secret; but its main points soon became public. The report, declassified, was reprinted by the Joint Committee on Defense Production, 94th Congress, 2d Session, 1976.

30. Ibid., p. 24.

31. Rearden, *The Evolution of American Strategic Doctrine,* pp. 45–46.

32. Ibid., pp. 52, 78.

33. Kahn's best-known work was the voluminous *On Thermonuclear War* (Princeton, N.J.: Princeton University Press, 1960). Two subsequent books, although somewhat anticlimactic, were notable for their reiteration and elaboration of Kahn's basic ideas: *Thinking About the Unthinkable* (New York: Horizon Press, 1962) and *On*

Escalation: Metaphor and Scenarios (New York: Praeger Publishers, 1965). After Kahn's death in July 1983, his colleagues at Hudson published a book he had almost completed: *Thinking About the Unthinkable in the 1980s* (New York: Simon and Schuster, 1984). Representative of other maximalist views on controlled strategic war was Klaus Knorr's sober and balanced exploration of the subject in Knorr and Read, *Limited Strategic War*, ch. 1, and Glenn H. Snyder's well-rounded analysis in his seminal book, *Deterrence and Defense: Toward a Theory of National Security* (Princeton, N.J.: Princeton University Press, 1961), pp. 193–224.

34. In his Ann Arbor speech, which closely followed the ideas of his adviser and speechwriter William Kaufmann, McNamara said, "The U.S. has come to the conclusion that to the extent feasible, basic military strategy in a possible general nuclear war should be approached in much the same way that more conventional military operations have been regarded in the past. That is to say, principal military objectives, in the event of a nuclear war stemming from a major attack on the Alliance, should be the destruction of the enemy's military forces, not of his civilian population. . . . In other words, we are giving a possible opponent the strongest imaginable incentive to refrain from striking our own cities." See William W. Kaufmann, *The McNamara Strategy* (New York: Harper and Row, 1964), p. 117.

35. Eisenhower, like Dulles, was concerned that if the allies were not given an equal, or at least larger, share in the operation of nuclear weapons to deter Soviet aggression against them, they would either go the French and British route or move toward neutrality. Although domestic and foreign opposition dissuaded Eisenhower from pushing for an independent European nuclear force, he went so far as to favor a change in U.S. atomic secrecy laws that would permit the allies to gain custody of nuclear weapons. In explaining this position to a reporter, he said, "I have always been of the belief that we should not deny to our allies . . . what your potential enemy already has. We do want allies to be treated as partners and allies, and not as junior members of a firm who are to be seen but not heard." See *New York Times*, February 4, 1960, p. 12.

36. Kahn, *On Escalation*, pp. 264–269.

37. On the United States' consideration of nuclear sharing as a means of dealing with the problem of nuclear proliferation in the late 1950s, see Robert E. Osgood, *NATO: The Entangling Alliance* (Chicago: University of Chicago Press, 1962), pp. 216–237.

38. Kaufmann's review of Kissinger's *Nuclear Weapons and Foreign Policy* (New York: Harper & Row, 1957) was a particularly devastating criticism of relying upon tactical nuclear weapons as a substitute for conventional resistance and, especially, of Kissinger's effort to adapt such weapons to limited warfare. See William W. Kaufmann, "The Crisis in Military Affairs," *World Politics*, vol. 10 (July 1958), 579–603.

39. See Thornton Read's exposition of this view in Knorr and Read, *Limited Strategic War*, ch. 3 ("Limited Strategic War and Tactical Nuclear War").

40. Kissinger expounded his strategy of limited nuclear war in some detail, including references to small self-contained, airborne, mobile tactical units and to the avoidance of industrial targets and the largest population centers, in *Nuclear Weapons and Foreign Policy* (New York: Harper and Row, 1957), ch. 7. By 1960, however, having concluded that the military had failed to find a convincing method of fighting such a war, he abandoned the idea. See Henry Kissinger, "Limited War: Nuclear or Conventional—A Reappraisal," in Brennan, *Arms Control, Disarmament, and National Security*, pp. 138–152; originally published in *Daedalus*, vol. 89 (Fall 1960), 800–817.

41. Citing the United States' irremediable vulnerability to a Soviet retaliatory blow, Kissinger declared that, despite his countless reassurances to the European allies about Washington's nuclear commitment to them, "if my analysis is correct we must face the fact that it is absurd to base the strategy of the West on the credibility of the threat of mutual suicide." Several sentences later, after challenging the political feasibility and credibility of carrying out such a threat, he continued: "And therefore I would say, which I might not say in office, the European allies should not keep asking us to multiply strategic assurances that we cannot possibly mean, or if we do mean, we should not want to execute because if we execute, we risk the destruction of civilization." See "NATO: The Next Thirty Years," *Survival*, vol. 21 (November/December, 1979), 266. Even more categorical in its renunciation of nuclear first-use was former Secretary of Defense McNamara's statement in an article in *Foreign Affairs* in 1983: "Having spent seven years as Secretary of Defense dealing with the problems unleashed by the initial nuclear chain reaction 40 years ago, I do not believe we can avoid serious and unacceptable risk of nuclear war until we recognize—and until we base all our military plans, defense budgets, weapon deployments, and arms negotiations on the recognition—that *nuclear weapons serve no military purpose whatsoever. They are totally useless—*

except only to deter one's opponent from using them" (italics in original). He went on to say (in a statement of questionable historical accuracy) that, in private conversations with Presidents Kennedy and Johnson, he had "recommended, without qualification, that they never initiate, under any circumstances, the use of nuclear weapons. I believe they accepted my recommendation." See Robert S. McNamara, "The Military Role of Nuclear Weapons: Perceptions and Misperceptions," *Foreign Affairs*, vol. 62 (Fall 1983), 79.

42. See Fred Ikle, "NATO's First Nuclear Use: A Deepening Trap?" *Strategic Review* (Winter 1980), pp. 18–23. In its analysis of the problem, William Kaufmann's critique of nuclear first-use was essentially the same as Ikle's. Kaufmann, too, advocated a no-nuclear first-use posture rather than a declaration of policy, but his pre-scription, in addition to some tactical and organizational measures to strengthen conventional forces, was to create a separate, mobile, retaliatory tactical nuclear force, out of the way of conventional forces (see John D. Steinbruner, Leon V. Sigal, eds., *Alliance Security: NATO and the No-First-Use Question* [Washington, D.C.: Brookings Institution, 1983], chs. 3 and 4).

43. Kahn, *Thinking About the Unthinkable in the 1980s*, p. 31.

44. Ibid., pp. 140, 212, 218.

45. McGeorge Bundy, George F. Kennan, Robert S. McNamara, and Gerard Smith, "Nuclear Weapons and the Atlantic Alliance," *Foreign Affairs*, vol. 60 (Spring 1982), 753–768.

46. See Richard K. Betts, "NATO Deterrence Doctrine: No Way Out," CISA Working Paper No. 51, Center for International and Strategic Affairs, University of California, Los Angeles, June 1985. Betts can be located in the middle of the maximalist/minimalist spectrum. Robert Jervis, marshaling all the arguments of the min-imalists, makes the rationality of strategic illogic the theme of his critique of "countervailing strategy," which would base deterrence on denying the Soviets military advantage from any kind of aggres-sion. See Robert Jervis, *The Illogic of American Nuclear Strategy* (Ithaca, N.Y.: Cornell University Press, 1984).

47. The most comprehensive treatments of the ABM debate are Ernest J. Yanarella, *The Missile Defense Controversy* (Lexington: Uni-versity of Kentucky Press, 1977), and Benson D. Adams, *Ballistic Missile Defense* (New York: American Elsevier, 1971).

48. See, for example, Joseph Coffey's passing mention of this argument in his balanced analysis of the ABM debate, in "The Anti-Ballistic Missile Debate," *Foreign Affairs*, vol. 45 (April 1967), 411.

49. Donald G. Brennan, "The Case for Missile Defense," *Foreign Affairs*, vol. 47 (April 1969), 433–448.

50. See Richard Nixon, *U.S. Foreign Policy for the 1970's, I* (February 18, 1970), p. 122. The next year's report to Congress, in elaborating the "doctrine of strategic sufficiency," indicated not only that it was necessary to have flexible nuclear responses beyond a finite capacity to inflict unacceptable destruction but also that the capabilities for such responses should not convey the impression to the Soviet Union of threatening a disarming attack. Further endorsing the minimalist approach, the report stated, "The United States and the Soviet Union have now reached a point where small numerical advantages in strategic forces have little military relevance. The attempt to obtain large advantages would spark an arms race which would, in the end, prove pointless" (*U.S. Foreign Policy for the 1970's, II* [February 25, 1971], p. 171).

51. See Harold Brown, *Department of Defense Annual Report, FY 1981* (January 29, 1980), pp. 65–68. Two authoritative explanations of the meaning of PD-59 and the countervailing strategy can be found in Leon Sloss and Marc Dean Millot, "U.S. Nuclear Strategy in Evolution," *Strategic Review*, vol. 12 (Winter 1984), 19–28, and in Walter Slocombe, "The Countervailing Strategy," *International Security*, vol. 5 (Spring 1981), 18–27. See also Harold Brown's testimony in "Nuclear War Strategy," *Hearings, Committee on Foreign Relations*, U.S. Senate, 96th Congress, 2d Session, September 16, 1980.

52. Representative of the reasoned opposition to flexible and controlled nuclear responses was Herbert ("Pete") Scoville's article "Flexible Madness," in which he defended existential MAD principally by criticizing flexible response as costly, futile, illusory, provocative, and dangerous. The new elaboration of controlled counterforce strategy, he argued, was "an open-ended justification for new, expensive programs." It was a rationale for improved silo-killing missiles, which "must inevitably look to the Russians like an attempt to acquire a first-strike counterforce capability against their ICBMs," and which would lead both sides to put ICBMs on a risky hair-trigger alert for launch on warning. Strategic sense, he concluded, lay in making deterrence as effective as possible, not in hedging against its failure. On the subject of moral rectitude, he declared: "It is probably more moral to prevent slaughter by threatening disaster than to facilitate limited death and destruction." See *Foreign Policy* (Spring 1974), pp. 164–177.

53. These and other qualifications were most fully stated in the *Department of Defense Annual Report: FY 1982* (January 16, 1981). Regarding decapitation, this report noted that "we must, and do, include options to target organs of Soviet political and military leadership and control. . . . At the same time, of course, we recognize the role that a surviving supreme command could and would play in the termination of hostilities, and can envisage many scenarios in which destruction of them would be inadvisable and contrary to our own best interests" (ibid., pp. 41–42). Brown sets forth an equally discriminating retrospective defense of PD-59 in his book *Thinking About National Security: Defense and Foreign Policy in a Dangerous World* (Boulder, Colo.: Westview, 1983), pp. 79–83.

54. *Department of Defense Annual Report: FY 1981* (January 29, 1980), p. 67.

55. For representative arguments along these lines, see the statements by James R. Schlesinger and William R. Van Cleave in "ABM Revisited: Promise or Peril?" *The Washington Quarterly*, vol. 4 (Autumn 1981), 53–85. See also William Schneider, Jr., et al., *U.S. Strategic-Nuclear Policy and Ballistic Missile Defense: The 1980s and Beyond*, Special Report, Institute of Foreign Policy Analysis, 1980.

56. Two long-time experts in the fields of defense and arms control, George W. Rathjens and Jack Ruina, present this view when they argue that "the current obscene destructive capability of each side is such that reducing it by 10 percent, 20 percent, or 50 percent would hardly make nuclear war less damaging. Moreover, the numbers themselves are not likely to cause either the Soviet Union or the United States to behave very differently in a crisis. Proposals for reductions should therefore be judged as encouraging indications that leaders on both sides explicitly acknowledge the futility of the arms race, and no longer conceive of arms control as a means to restructure nuclear forces so as to make them more or less usable. From this point of view, larger reductions are better than smaller ones. But regardless of what the reduction level may be, an opportunity for an agreement should not be foregone because of disproportionate attention to hypothetical nuclear threats or our excessive preoccupation with calculations of 'relative stability'" (*New York Times*, August 3, 1986, p. E23).

57. Colin S. Gray and Keith Payne, "Victory Is Possible," *Foreign Policy* (Summer 1980), 14–27.

58. Richard Halloran reported on this document at length and with numerous quotes in *New York Times*, May 30, 1982, pp. 1, 12.

59. *New York Times*, June 3, 1983, pp. 1, 34.

60. Spurgeon M. Keeny, Jr., and Wolfgang K.H. Panofsky, "MAD Versus NUTS: Can Doctrine or Weaponry Remedy the Mutual Hostage Relationship of the Superpowers?" *Foreign Affairs*, vol. 60 (Winter 1981/1982), 287–304.

61. Garfinkle, *The Politics of the Nuclear Freeze*.

62. The case for nuclear winter was most effectively popularized by the scientist Carl Sagan. See, for example, his article "Nuclear War and Climatic Catastrophe," *Foreign Affairs*, vol. 62 (Winter 1983/1984), 257–292. Sagan's views were widely challenged and remain quite controversial among scientists. For a useful summary of this controversy, see "The Nuclear Winter Debate," *Strategic Survey, 1984–1985* (London: IISS, 1985), pp. 23–27. Stanley L. Thompson and Stephen H. Schneider, in "Nuclear Winter Reappraised," *Foreign Affairs*, vol. 64 (Summer 1986), 981–1005, are skeptical about a global "threshold" of ecological damage and a "global freeze" but point out the many uncertainties, depending on the nature of war scenarios. Less controversial are the great difficulties of imposing positive political control and limitation on the use of nuclear weapons. See Paul Bracken's well-informed analysis: *The Command and Control of Nuclear Forces* (New Haven, Conn.: Yale University Press, 1983); David Ford's popular critique: *The Button: The Pentagon's Command and Control System—Does It Work?* (New York: Simon and Schuster, 1985); and Bruce G. Blair's sounder version of the subject, *Strategic Command and Control: Redefining the Nuclear Threat* (Washington, D.C.: The Brookings Institution, 1985).

63. National Conference of Catholic Bishops, *The Challenge of Peace: God's Promise and Our Response,* a Pastoral Letter on War and Peace, May 3, 1983.

64. *New York Times,* April 27, 1986, pp. 1, 34.

65. Jonathan Schell, *The Fate of the Earth* (New York: Alfred A. Knopf, 1982), p. 95.

66. Jonathan Schell, *The Abolition* (New York: Alfred A. Knopf, 1984), Part II: "A Deliberate Policy."

67. On the technology and international politics of the conventionalization of nuclear functions, see Carl H. Builder, *The Prospects and Implications of Non-Nuclear Means for Strategic Conflict,* Adelphi Papers, No. 200 (Summer, 1985).

68. This case is made by Albert Carnesale and Charles Glaser in "ICBM Vulnerability: The Cures Are Worse Than the Disease," *International Security,* vol. 7 (Summer 1982), 70–85. To the valid objection of maximalists, however, the authors, like a number of other minimalists, include among their prescriptions "improvements

in the capabilities and survivability of space-based and earth-based sensors and C^3I equipment in order to provide a credible option for launch-under-attack with minimum risk of false alarm" (ibid., p. 84).

69. William V. O'Brien makes the most balanced case for the application of just-war principles to the conduct of nuclear war in Chapter 7 ("The Failure of Deterrence") of William V. O'Brien and John Langan, eds., *The Nuclear Dilemma and the Just War Tradition* (Lexington, Mass.: Lexington Books, 1986).

70. Both Herman Kahn and Thomas Schelling have briefly addressed the issue of war termination in their writings. Several other books have been devoted to the subject as well: Paul Kecskemeti, *Strategic Surrender: The Politics of Victory and Defeat* (Stanford, Calif.: Stanford University Press, 1958); Fred C. Ikle, *Every War Must End* (New York: Columbia University Press, 1971); Nissan Oren, ed., *Termination of Wars: Processes, Procedures, and Aftermaths* (Jerusalem: The Magnes Press, Hebrew University, 1982); and Clark C. Abt, *A Strategy for Terminating a Nuclear War* (Boulder, Colo.: Westview Press, 1985).

71. See Albert Wohlstetter's two-part article in *Foreign Policy:* "Is There a Strategic Arms Race?" (Summer 1974), 3–20, and (Fall 1974), 48–81.

72. The single most salient debate on this issue is the lengthy exchange of views between Albert Wohlstetter and his critics and supporters in "Morality and Deterrence," *Commentary* (December 1983), 4–22. This exchange follows Wohlstetter's article "Bishops, Statesmen, and Other Strategists on the Bombing of Innocents," *Commentary* (June 1983), 15–35. The debate makes it clear that insofar as differences of moral evaluation in this debate have hinged on different assessments of the relationship of means to consequences—as has certainly been true to a great extent, although philosophical and subjective preferences obviously color pragmatic arguments—the critical disagreement pertains to the feasibility of significantly limiting and controlling the use of nuclear weapons so that nuclear means will be effective in achieving the intended consequences and both the means and the ends will be proportionate to the value of the political purpose of a nuclear response, to which no better alternative response is available.

Index

p 11 – 14, 20 33